# BUSINESS *THE*
# amazon.com
# WAY

**SECRETS** of the World's
Most Astonishing Web Business

## REBECCA SAUNDERS

CAPSTONE

Copyright © Rebecca Saunders 1999

The right of Rebecca Saunders to be identified as the author of this work has been asserted in accordance with the Copyright, Designs and Patents Act 1988

First published 1999 by
Capstone US
Business Books Network
163 Central Avenue
Suite 2
Hopkins Professional Building
Dover
NH 03820
USA

Capstone Publishing Limited
Oxford Centre for Innovation
Mill Street
Oxford OX2 0JX
United Kingdom
http://www.capstone.co.uk

British Library Cataloguing in Publication Data
A CIP catalogue record for this book is available from the British Library

US Library of Congress Cataloging-in-Publication Data
A CIP catalog record for this book is available from the US Library of Congress

ISBN 1-84112-054-5

Typeset in 11/15 pt New Baskerville by
Sparks Computer Solutions Ltd, Oxford
http://www.sparks.co.uk
Printed and bound by
T.J. International Ltd, Padstow, Cornwall

This book is printed on acid-free paper

Substantial discounts on bulk quantities of Capstone books are available to corporations, professional associations and other organizations. If you are in the USA or Canada, phone the LPC Group for details on (1-800-626-4330) or fax (1-800-243-0138). Everywhere else, phone Capstone Publishing on (+44-1865-798623) or fax (+44-1865-240941).

# CONTENTS

At the very least, Jeff Bezos, founder and CEO of Amazon.com, has proved that you can get rich doing business on the Web. While his company has yet to make a profit, as money is reinvested into growing the business, his ten secrets of launching a cyberstore are a blueprint for entrepreneurs who would wish to do likewise and for managers in traditional businesses who see the Web as a new channel of business.

Bezos saw an opportunity that others, even those in the book industry, failed to see, but he saw it because he knew the potential of the Web. There's still room for more ventures but only for those who are willing to ground their idea for a business model that won't work in the real world but will work on the Internet with knowhow on e-commerce.

Bezos has assembled a team of talented "nerds," and he has found a way to keep them at a time when such expertise is highly prized, not only by literally giving them a piece of his dream but also by giving them an opportunity we all would like from our jobs: to change the world in a fundamental way.

The business of Amazon.com has changed dramatically since the cyberstore was launched but its focus continues to be the same: to be the world's biggest store on the net. There are many small issues that can distract but Bezos has a clarity of purpose that allows him to practise triage when the need arises.

From cyberbuzz, to an integrative marketing effort, to ensuring there is performance behind the image, Bezos has built a brand name that is recognized both off and on the Web.

Bezos knows that it's easy for another Webstore to underprice him, so he has built his cyberstore on value-added services.

The service chain that builds customer loyalty to Amazon.com includes not only use of the Internet as a sales channel but mastery of distribution channels to provide safe and quick delivery.

All retail operations have to deal with razor-thin profit margin – even those on the Web. But to make the economic model for his business work, money has to go into expansion – which means practising frugality as a value. But it has also given him a reputation for eccentricity.

Technological advances can give you a competitive advantage off- and online, but in real time or not, you have to remember that technological innovations are usually short lived; consequently, practising technoleverage is an ongoing responsibility. On the Web, however, technoleverage is essential merely for survival as a cyberstore.

From editorial content improvements to process changes to strategic shifts, such changes are essential to counter competitive moves and continue to meet customer expectations.

Bezos has used alliances, partnerships, and acquisitions to grow business at his cyberstore and opportunities for the future.

# PREFACE

As I write this book, I am continuously checking the financial sections of local newspapers in both anticipation and fear of the next move on Jeff Bezos' part to achieve the expanded mission of Amazon.com: "to become the world's largest …" Knowing that I'm writing this book, friends ask me if Amazon.com will make a profit within the next six months or year, and they ask me to predict his next move, but I honestly do not know. If I did, I would not be sitting here at all odd hours of the day and night writing about this business pioneer. I can only say, based on my many years in business reporting, that Jeff Bezos, as CEO of Amazon.com, would seem to be doing everything right in running a young but growing company on the Web.

Many authors dangle suggestions that they have secret insights that they will hold off sharing until the sequel. I have none – for now. Like Will Rodgers, "All I know is what I read in the papers." And magazines, and on his and others' Web sites. I have never personally interviewed Jeff Bezos. Since I started this book, he has been too busy doing what a CEO of a fledgling business should be doing: focusing on the business of growing the company. While I am disappointed I have not yet spoken to him, I believe it has made this assessment of his leadership strengths more objective.

Over the years, I have interviewed numerous CEOs and I have found them to possess charisma and communication skills that were critical to their success but that made it tough during a single visit to make an unbiased assessment of their leadership practices.

Will there be a sequel? There should be. The story of Amazon.com likely will be twofold. As Bezos himself has said, the company is currently in an "investing mode," suitable words for a former money manager. The rest of the story – of the "harvesting phase," as Bezos has called it – will be equally insightful. But as entrepreneurs look to the Web to make their dream of a business a reality – and established companies scramble on the Web to be there before equivalent upstarts in their field take them on, as Amazon.com stole the march on the major book chains – there are lessons about e-commerce and entrepreneurialism that can be learned from reading this book.

What have Bezos' competitors done wrong that has allowed him to reach the point his firm is currently at? Interestingly, they have done nothing wrong from a management perspective other than to underestimate the speed by which the Web would grow to become a major competitor to traditional retail. At present, the rabbit would seem to be ahead of the turtle.

If I have any complaint about those in publishing, it is to question why an idea like Amazon.com came from those outside of publishing. Were we too close to see? If this preface is to contain any management insights, it may be that – for both entrepreneurs and those progressive businesspeople who wish to mine the opportunities of e-commerce.

For those of you in traditional businesses, it is important that you do not become complacent about your firm's position, whatever the external development. You must forever be looking about you both to identify customer demands and to determine how to reach those customers. For those of you who picked up this book because you want to be like Bezos, found a company on the Web, and one day become a multimillionaire, let me repeat a comment I make in this book: "The Web allows entrepreneurs to do what wouldn't work in the real world." The opportunities would seem limited only by your imagination and business acumen.

*Rebecca Saunders*

Introduction

# THE SAM WALTON OF THE WEB

"The best way to predict the future is to invent it."
**– Alan Kay, Director of Research, Apple Computer Co., from *Creating Excellence* by Hickman and Silva**

The personalities of entrepreneurs influence the success of the organizations they found. The nature of a business may affect how it is run, but the tenaciousness of the entrepreneur behind it determines how well it is run and whether it survives – even if a business is just an upstart in a crowded market. But for an organization that is cutting new ground like Amazon.com, the Seattle-based e-tailer, its success stems from the audacity of the idea as well as the execution of that idea, and the leadership skills of the person behind both: Jeff Bezos.

## 1995: AMAZON.COM GOES ON STREAM

Launched as a Web site in July 1995, Amazon.com Inc. by the start of 1999 had a market valuation of $6 billion, more than the combined value of Barnes and Noble, and Borders, its biggest book store competitors online and off. Net sales for the fourth quarter of 1998 were $252.9 million, an increase of 283 percent over net sales of $66.0 million for the fourth quarter of 1997. But the company continues to be the subject of discussion at business breakfasts and lunches by current and potential investors, Web watchers, and of course investment managers. In early 1999 the stock was trading at around $209 a share, 23 times its May 1997 initial public offering price of $9 a share, although the organization has yet to make a profit. The irrepressible Bezos has projected that his company will reach $1 billion in annual sales by 2000. He won't tell when he expects his company to make a profit, but early investors were told not to expect dividends for at least five years. Most investors continue to have faith in Bezos, as does David Gardner, author of *The Motley Fool Investment Guide*. He told reporters that had Bezos wanted Amazon profitable, it would be but it would only be a small company. On the other hand, Gardner, considered a Bezos fan, admitted that if Amazon did not make a profit in another two years or eight quarters, "it would be in trouble." [For other money managers' viewpoints, see the box in this chapter.]

# AN EXPANDED VISION FOR AMAZON.COM

Clearly Bezos has a plan but he considers it his business and not that of the business press. That he has had to make course corrections in response to customer needs and competitor actions only makes it more difficult to scout out the fullness of that plan. He has denied rumors that he would like to build a megastore online that could take on real-world Wal-Mart, and he has laughed when members of the press have asked if he plans to make Amazon.com into a portal, yet he has also told the same business press that management visions change. Certainly expansion of the retail site's line of products beyond books to include videos, CDs and links to purchase pharmaceuticals, pet supplies and groceries, auctions and even greetings cards, suggests Bezos may, indeed, want to make Amazon.com an online Wal-Mart, or the economics of e-retail may demand this growth to ensure profits. But obviously Amazon.com is no longer just an online bookstore. Bezos is likely to have the same impact that Sears' catalog had on the retail industry, and his online store may grow into the Sears or Woolworth of the new millennium.

# GOING PUBLIC

As this book will show, Jeff Bezos has numerous management and leadership skills. One is clearly his ability to address successfully various constituencies, from customers to employees, to investors and the business community. His success in dealing with the press was first evident in March 1997 when he offered 2.5 million shares of common stock for sale. To those who wonder how stock sales were able to soar, this is the answer. Less than a year before, his site had appeared on the front page of *The Wall Street Journal*. And in subsequent interviews, Bezos milked it for all he was worth. As James Romenesko of *Knight-Ridder/Tribune Business* observed, Bezos couldn't have asked for a better way to introduce himself to the business community and investors, many of whom were anxious to put money into any potentially successful company associated with ties to the Internet. Eager to mine the potential of this latest virgin territory for businesses, comparable to the men and women who rushed to California during the gold rush to find their fortunes, business investors couldn't wait to find an opportunity to plonk down their money to be a part of this new thing they were hearing about called e-commerce. Not only did The *Journal* story call Amazon.com "an underground sensation for thousands of book-lovers around the world," but it suggested that its success was due to Bezos'

> "To do something a little bit crazy, you have to be very optimistic, and I was. I always expected Amazon.com to be very successful. But what's unusual is that it has vastly outpaced my expectations in terms of how big a company it's become."
> **Bezos, 1997**

understanding of Web technology "like no other retailer." Subsequent stories played up Bezos' knowledge but they also made him seem endearing, with economic necessities of a startup business – like desks made from oversized doors and two by fours – sounding like amusing eccentricities, that we couldn't help but want to see this "David" overcome the "Goliaths" of big business.

Most important, Amazon.com appeared in numerous publications as an online success story, as journalist Romenesko observed at that time, despite the fact that it hadn't yet made a profit. The business stories, combined with the romance of being able to invest in the latest business frontier, and the attractiveness of financially supporting a likeable young man with a dream, were enough to raise the bookstore's shares to premium rates – initially offered at $15 a share, the day closed with trading at $23.50.

> Stephen Segaller has said that Ann Winblad described Amazon.com's initial impact on other book chains as "like a deer in the headlights."

Money managers were divided on the company's worth, and the questions continue to exist, but Bezos, a former money manager himself, has devoted considerable effort to sustain credibility in him by investors. As Charles J. Fombrun, in his book *Reputation: Realizing Value from the Corporate Image*, suggests, organizations' reputations have economic value that translate into investor interest. To investors, he writes, "the currency of exchange is credibility" – less of the organization as a whole as that of the organization's leader. So public statements by Bezos in the early years of the company were critical to set expectations of money managers, and subsequent stories in the press have had the purpose of demonstrating promises kept, from brand enhancement to continuous technological development, to expanded services and value to customers. Take this one: "Our goal is to make the shopping experience a pleasant one for our customers."

Cornered about the issue of profitability, Bezos told one reporter, "We're focusing on introducing ourselves to customers. To do anything else right now would be a very poor management decision. It's not at all unusual for a four-year-old company to be in an investment cycle rather than a harvest cycle. What is unusual," he continued, "is for such companies to be publicly traded, but even that is not unique." Bezos went on to make an analogy with biotech firms and public support for them. "They've supported us," he concluded, "because the Internet has created an opportunity for companies to build brand names far more quickly than has been historically possible, which means that everything else happens far more quickly, too."

## THE "AHA" MOMENT

Bezos is expansive on many of his plans but not on his ultimate goal for Amazon.com. But some clarity may come from the story of the founding of Amazon.com.

Hearing about it, the startup sounds very much like the script of a sit-com or a two-hour made-for-TV movie. That the end result can be watched on a screen that sits on a desk or table – albeit a computer monitor, not a TV – may be partially responsible for the analogy, but it's the audacity of the hero – and nuttiness of the story – that make it seem like it could be the product of a TV writer's imagination. Jeff Bezos, a young man in his early thirties (think Jimmy Stewart or Chevy Chase), chooses to leave a well-paying job on Wall Street and, with his wife and dog, drives West to set up an online retail business, developing a business plan on his laptop while his wife drives their dated Chevy Blazer.

Flashback two months: it's April 1994 and our hero, Jeff Bezos, a hedge fund manager in New York City, is surfing the Internet when he comes upon a statistic: Web usage is growing at 2300 percent monthly. Others might be intrigued but do nothing about it. Not Bezos, who holds a secret wish one day to build a business on the Web.

He has used the term "compelled" to describe his emotional reaction to that factoid. If he hadn't acted immediately, he has said, he would have regretted it his whole life: "When something is growing that fast, every second counts." He told one reporter, "I decided that when I was 80 I wouldn't regret quitting a Wall Street job when I was 30, but when I was 80 I might really regret missing this great opportunity."

## EARLY SIGNS OF ENTREPRENEURIALISM AND NERDNESS

Bezos' response could have been anticipated. Already his fascination with technology was evident. Likewise, his entrepreneurial instincts. Sam Walton, founder of Wal-Mart, wrote in his book *Made in America* that people assumed that Wal-Mart was something dreamed up out of the blue when

Walton was middle aged. Not so. His first store and each thereafter were an outgrowth, he says, of his "being unable to leave
well enough alone, another experiment." Likewise Bezos. At
the age of 14, he has admitted to wanting to be an astronaut or
a physicist, or something that would allow him to use cutting-
edge technology. The family garage was reportedly filled with
Bezos' early efforts at engineering. In high school, he founded
his first firm, DREAM Institute, a summer school program to
stimulate creative thinking in youngsters, and he made money
from it, even charging his brother and sister to attend. In ma-
joring in engineering and computer sciences at Princeton, from
which he graduated *summa cum laude*, he was following in his
father's and grandfather's steps: his father was an engineer for
Exxon and his grandfather was a manager for the Atomic En-
ergy Commission. Following graduation, Bezos joined FITEL,
a high-tech startup company. After that he joined Bankers Trust
where he helped lead development of computer systems that
played a role in managing $150-plus billion in assets.

## OFF TO ...

Within two months of reading about the Web's sales potential,
Bezos had quit his job at D. E. Shaw & Company, and he and
his wife had packed their furnishings in a van and were head-
ing west but, as corporate lore says, unclear where they would
settle. Bezos had identified 20 products that could be sold on
the Internet, then thoroughly investigated the market situation of the top five: books, CDs, videos, and computer hardware
and software (which, interestingly enough, are now all available either directly or indirectly on his site). Of most concern
to Bezos, he has said, was the size of the relative markets. Price
point was another factor for consideration. He was looking for

a low-priced product to offset customer fears about purchasing online. Finally, he wanted a product for which there was a range of choices. He finally selected books because (1) book retail is a $82 billion market; (2) books are low-priced, and (3) book titles number worldwide about 3 million. Yet he wasn't sure where he would settle. He had four likely locations: Portland, Oregon; Lake Tahoe, Nevada; Boulder, Colorado; and Seattle, Washington. He recognized that he would need a state without a state tax, with a large high-tech workforce and proximity to a major book distributor. So westward went Bezos, his wife, and the family dog, with instructions to the moving van drivers with the family's belongings to call him on the cell phone for directions. Halfway across the country, Bezos recalls, he chose Seattle, which is the location of book distributor Ingram, which continues to provide 60 percent of the organization's books.

En route, the cell phone was also used to locate seed money and to find a vice president of product development for the brand-new company, or so the early story of the founding goes.

Once in Seattle, Bezos and his first three employees set up computers in the garage where they started writing the software that was critical to Amazon.com's launch. There was also time spent at fund-raising. Bezos, the future founder of an online bookstore, has admitted that much of this took place at the coffee shop of his local Barnes and Noble, which is ironic since it is Amazon's major book competitor today.

## LOOKING FOR MONEY IN THE RIGHT PLACES

The business plan brought two venture capitalists, perhaps literally to the negotiating table: Kleiner Perkins Caulfield & Byers, and Humber Winblad. Despite his contacts in New York City's money markets, Bezos had to turn to Silicon Valley for funding for his upstart firm. At the time firms in the east weren't as interested in technology investments as those out west, according to a Coopers & Lybrand study, which found west coast firms investing more than three times the amount in Internet startups as their east coast counterparts.

John Doerr of Kleiner Perkins won out in negotiations to fund Amazon, but insights into those early discussions come from Ann Winblad, in the book *Nerds: A Brief History of the Internet* by Stephen Segaller. In it, Winblad recalls that Bezos said, "I know nothing about the book industry. Nothing. I want to tell you that up front. But let me just tell you this: I know that I can get the books here, and I can get them to the customers and forget about bricks and mortar." By selling on the Internet, he told Winblad, he would change the economics of the book industry as a whole. She believes that he has done just that.

## ABRACADABRA: AMAZON.COM

In June 1995 Amazon.com Books Inc. became a reality on the Web. Bezos liked the name Cadabra (as in Abra …), but friends pointed to the similarity with another word, "cadaver," so Amazon it became. Ever conscious of the value of branding on the Web, Bezos chose to name his site after the world's largest river, telling newsgroups that Amazon.com, in turn, would become the biggest bookstore in the world. Despite the Web site's impressive sounding name, however, those first few weeks found Bezos doing the grunt work, loading and unloading packages

# THE LIFE AND TIMES OF JEFF BEZOS

◆ **1986:** graduates from Princeton University, *summa cum laude*, Phi Beta Kappa, with a BS in Electrical Engineering & Computer Science

◆ **1986–1988:** employed by FITEL, New York city-based high-tech startup

◆ **1988–1990:** employed by Bankers Trust Company

◆ **1990–1994:** employed by D. E. Shaw & Co.

◆ **July 1994:** Jeff Bezos founds Amazon.com

◆ **June 1995:** Bezos launches Amazon.com Inc. on Web

◆ **February 1997:** Barnes and Noble goes online

◆ **May 1997:** Amazon.com goes public

◆ **July 1997:** Amazon.com enters into agreement with Yahoo!

◆ **July 1997:** Amazon.com becomes exclusive bookseller for Excite

◆ **September 1997:** Amazon.com becomes exclusive bookseller on Prodigy shopping network

◆ **October 1997:** Amazon.com becomes exclusive bookseller on Alta Vista

◆ **October 1997:** Amazon.com and Netscape announce strategic online deal

◆ **November 1997:** Amazon.com and @Home Network sign agreement

◆ **November 1997:** Amazon opens second distribution center

◆ **December 1997:** Amazon.com and GeoCities strike exclusive bookseller agreement

◆ **December 1997:** Amazon.com completes $74 million credit facility

◆ **February 1998:** Amazon.com Associates Member Program surpasses 30,000 members

◆ **March 1998:** Amazon.com Kids goes online

◆ **May 1998:** Amazon.com acquires Bookpages and Telebook to expand in the UK, and Internet movie database

◆ **June 1998:** Amazon.com opens music store

◆ **July 1998:** Amazon.com establishes relationship with Intuit's personal finance Web site and select desktop software

◆ **August 1998:** Amazon buys PlanetAll and Junglee Corporation

◆ **September 1998:** Amazon.com and Yahoo! strike Global Merchant Agreement

◆ **October 1998:** Amazon.com enters European book market

◆ **November 1998:** Microsoft signs Amazon.com as Premier Merchant on MSN shopping

◆ **November 1998:** Amazon.com adds videos and other gift items

◆ **December 1998:** Cyberian outpost joins product retailers on Amazon.com's new shopping referral service

◆ **January 1999:** Amazon.com opens third distribution center to meet rapid growth

◆ **January 1999:** Amazon.com reports Internet shoppers came in record numbers for holiday shopping

◆ **February 1999:** Amazon.com purchases interest in DrugStore.com

◆ **February 1999:** Amazon.com invests in DrugStore.com

◆ **March 1999:** Amazon.com invests in Pets.com

◆ **March 1999:** Amazon.com launches online auction site

◆ **April 1999:** Amazon.com agrees to purchase LiveBid.com, Internet provider of live auctions

◆ **April 1999:** Amazon.com adds Kansas distribution center to handle rapid growth

◆ **April 1999:** Amazon.com luanches greeting-card service

◆ **May 1999:** Amazon.com invests in HomeGrocer.com

◆ **May 1999:** Amazon.com announces plans to expand ditribution network to meed rapid growth.

in the back of his Blazer and delivering them to the post office himself.

## THE LAST FOUR YEARS

Much has happened in the four years since. When Amazon.com first entered the market, it had no big online rivals and there were no dominant traditional players. The number one supplier – Barnes and Noble – had only about one-tenth of market share and no online presence. While there is now a bevy of booksellers on the net, including book behemoth Barnes and Noble and second-largest bookseller Borders, Amazon has had the advantage of being there first. But as it has moved into new product lines like CDs and videos and now toiletries, pet supplies and groceries, and provides services like auctions and greetings cards, it has found itself up against dominant players in their markets, off and online or both. Yes, today, it may be the post office that sends trucks out to pick up deliveries from Amazon's warehouse, and others who do the loading and unloading, but analysts wonder if the organization can keep plowing funds back into the business without getting anything back. Money managers estimate that next year the online retailer will spend $200 million on marketing, a 50 percent increase.

> Bezos told a venture capitalist, "I will change the economics of the book industry as a whole."

Who cares that Amazon still hasn't made a profit? For the public record, Bezos says that he doesn't. He has expressed more concern that focus on profitability could distract management attention from the more critical business, which is, in his opinion, introducing each day more and more customers to Amazon.com. He sees Amazon right now in what he has called "an investment phase," not unusual for a firm having only recently celebrated its fourth birthday. The "harvesting cycle" will come later, he has said.

Some investment managers are less sanguine. Wary, they are telling their clients to sell. But those recommending that clients hold the course continue to outnumber them. These investors point to Amazon's head start on Web transactions, its ability to provide customized service, the endless selection of product within a few keystrokes of millions of customers, and access to technology that enables it to divine what other products customers might want – invaluable information in capturing new markets online. While it suffers from the liability of being a retailer, and consequently subject to the same razor-thin margins that all merchandisers must live with – they point to the fact that the retailer only need bring more customers to its single online site, not build stores of brick and mortar to raise sales, which represents a considerable cost to traditional retailers.

It is these economics, a product of being online, that is enabling Amazon to rewrite the retail industry. Like the impact that the arrival and growth of large retail giants like Sears, Roebuck and Company, J. C. Penney, and Montgomery Ward had on the mercantiles of the late 1890s and early 1900s, and later the impact that K-Mart, Target, and Wal-Mart had on the bottom line of these giant catalog companies, and still later the impact that category killers like Walgreen, Toys "R" Us, and The Home Depot have had on discount operations, Amazon.com has changed the economics of retail. Well aware of the role that Amazon.com is playing in e-commerce history,

Bezos supposedly daily takes photographs of his staff at work, creating a record for businesses that come after. He isn't being egotistical in his view of the role his firm is playing in history. In 1998, Amazon.com received top honors in the prestigious 1998 Computerworld Smithsonian Award competition, taking first place in Business and Related Services. The award recognizes those who have demonstrated vision and leadership in the innovative use of information technology. Amazon.com was said to be "a driving force behind e-retail, with technology that allows customers to find and purchase books in convenient and secure manner." Bezos said of the award: "We're flattered, of course, but more important this is recognition that online commerce has arrived. Millions of people, not just the digerati, are taking advantage of the benefits of secure online shopping."

Amazon.com is likely to become a classic case in e-commerce or, more appropriate, in e-retailing, and, as such, its startup and growth will be studied for years to come, as have Apple, Microsoft, Dell Computer and other technological innovators. But more interesting to those who would like to practise cybermarketing – either to supplement existing revenue or to build an Internet business – are the leadership secrets of Amazon's founder, Jeff Bezos.

## AN IDEA ALONE MEANS NOTHING

The success of Amazon.com does not stem solely from the underlying idea of an online store – not a bad idea in intself; the success of Amazon comes from implementation of that idea. Bezos believes likewise. In his opinion, it's easy to come up with ideas. It's the implementation that is hard. Most CEOs would agree. Those who have led strategic planning sessions have found items that appear on flip charts infrequently see the light of day. For CEOs all, Bezos has summed it up: "The hard part is putting them to work."

Bezos has earned Amazon its leading-edge status and success. His ten secrets:

◆ Secret #1: understand e-commerce. Amazon's founder studied the book market before choosing it as starting place for Amazon. But, more important, he understood the Internet. He has said that this know-how is Amazon's hard-earned advantage over barnesandnoble.com and Borders.com. As he faces competition from eBay and other online operations, this expertise should make for a level playing field.

> Bezos told reporter Lesley Hazleton, "I decided that when I was 80, I wouldn't regret quitting a Wall Street job when I was 30, but when I was 80 I might really regret missing this great opportunity."

◆ Secret #2: build an entrepreneurial team. Bezos has brought together a talented and diverse group of people. He has given them a challenge: to change the world in a fundamental way by making Amazon a success. And he has given them a sense of ownership of that mission, through generous stock-option incentives.

◆ Secret #3: focus. Bezos has articulated a mission but he isn't only talking about that. His actions exhibit a clarity of purpose that is allowing his young company to stay grounded as it goes through the turbulent transitions of growth and meets competitors head on. Bezos knows that there are many smaller issues that arise that can distract from that main goal, and he has had to practise triage to focus on those things that count most.

◆ Secret #4: brand the site. From the name he gave his site to his deals with other heavily trafficked Web sites that would channel users, to his ongoing investment in marketing, Bezos demonstrates how important branding is to e-commerce.

◆ Secret #5: get and keep customers by offering value. This means not only a discount on price, but a rich selection, customer retention through customized service, and fun. More still. You can offer price discounts, you can offer easy-to-use search and browse features, you can provide e-mail services, and you can secure Web-based credit card payment, but customers also want speedy delivery of their purchases.

◆ Secret #6: set up a distribution network. Bezos has opened four state-of-the-art distribution centers to shorten order-to-mailbox time for Amazon customers everywhere. Michael Porter talks about value chains for competitive advantage, and Amazon.com's chain includes not only use of the Internet as a sales channel but mastery of distribution channels to be able to better serve customers.

◆ Secret #7: practise frugality. Bezos runs a tight ship and with cause – that razor-thin profit margin. Bezos recognizes that by watching his overhead, he can spend much more on business expansion, which in e-commerce translates into more customers to his site.

◆ Secret #8: practise technoleverage. His brick-and-mortar competitors used superior inventory and ordering technology to overwhelm smaller retailers. Amazon now is rattling these same book sellers and other retailers with its on-line book reviewing and ordering system and other recently purchased technology, and continues to frighten, with its ownership of Junglee Corporation's search engine that permits on-line comparison shopping.

◆ Secret #9: constantly reinvent oneself. Enlightened imitation is necessary for Internet success. The rivalry between Amazon.com, the current leader, and barnesandnoble.com demonstrates the necessity of constant reinvention to achieve success. As Barnes and Noble launches television and advertising campaigns and duplicates Amazon's earlier tactics to draw customers to its site, Amazon has had to take countermeasures, expanding its offerings and acquiring technology companies like Junglee and PlanetAll and more recently DrugStore.com and an online pet supply store and supermarket. While extension of its product line has meant new competitors, it has also added to reason for customers to visit the site – which is necessary for the eventual profitability of Amazon.

◆ Secret #10: grow by strategic alliances as well as acquisitions. One year after launch, Amazon pioneered the concept of syndicated selling, and today it is linked with more than 60,000 sites, including five of the top six sites on the Web – AOL.com, Yahoo!, Netscape, GeoCities, and Excite – where visitors to these sites can purchase books from the Amazon.com catalog. Other deals have enabled Amazon to grow globally, expand its sales beyond books, differentiate itself from others online and off, and position itself for further growth.

# DIFFERENT VIEWS ON AMAZON.COM

Business reporters have gone to various investor managers for their view on Amazon.com. Here is a sampling from the press of money manager comments since Amazon.com first went public to present.

"Amazon has become the default name when you think of buying on the Net ... They are the poster child of Internet commerce."
**– Keith Benjamin, Internet analyst with BancAmerica Robertson Stephens, San Francisco, 1997**

On the difference between Amazon.com and Barnes and Noble: "The difference between the two is that Amazon.com is an insignificant speck in the book-selling universe. But it's a rapidly growing speck. Still book publishers are first going to take care of the people who sell billions of dollars of books, and that's Barnes & Noble." He then adds: "What Amazon has done better than any other Internet merchant is to take its store to the people. They've just cut deals with America Online and Yahoo!, so now they're weaving themselves more into the fabric of the Internet. Wherever you go on the Net, you will see an Amazon.com store. But they're going to be in a dogfight with Barnes & Noble."
**– Bill Bass, Analyst, Forrester Research, 1997**

"Despite the purchase, by Bertelsmann AG, of 50 percent of BarnesandNoble.com, and merger discussions among other sites to form 'online shopping networks,' I am confident Amazon remains the company to beat."
**– Peter Krasinovsky, Vice President of Arlen Communications, November 1998**

As Amazon.com adds each new product to its product line, it adds another competitor. Which prompted the following reference to it: "Amazon.toast."

**– George F. Colony, CEO, Forrester**

"Amazon can now control its own destiny and buy in on better prices."

**– Steve Lebow, Chairman, Global Retail Partners, Los Angeles, October 1998**

"Bezos will need the flexibility to step up his own delivery service and not rely totally on third parties."

**– Jay M. Tenenbaum, Chairman, CommerceNet (Trade Association of 500 Online Retailers)**

On Bezos's acquisition of Junglee and its future use, "There is a great chance for Amazon to become a destination site for a broad array of goods, whether they sell them or not. But consumers will demand a high level of integrity," as Amazon directs them to various Web sites.

**– Genni Combes, Analyst, Hambrecht & Quist, Inc.**

"I think the strategy is good. With the Internet, there are only so many ways to differentiate yourself to be big. Scale will rule. The more products you sell over the same cost structure, the more profitable you'll be."

**– Scott Appleby, Analyst, ABN Amro**

"To some people, once it became apparent that big chain superstores would jump on the Internet, they felt this is big trouble. But that hasn't been the case ... I think the reason Bezos will succeed, and it sounds very California, but it's karma. He remains very focused on delivering consumer value."

**– Jane Gardner, Group Management Supervisor and EVO at Foote, Cone & Belding, Amazon.com's Traditional- Media Agency**

About his branching out, "It's a question of identity. Amazon is known for its books and music business. Now it's going to become a shopping mall, too?"
**– David Simons of Digital Video Investments, New York**

"Amazon is focused – it is only interested in serving Internet clients. It doesn't have any other staff to worry about. High street stores understand retail but find it difficult to understand how technologies will impinge not just on them but on the economy generally. There just aren't many people out there who understand Internet retail."
**– Bud Margolis, Internet Retail Consultant, London, August 1998**

Pointing to how investors can get a personal feel for Amazon's prospects by trying it out, "His [Bezos'] greatest advantage is a lot of people who buy his stock buy his books."
**– Halsey Minor, CEO, CNET Inc., Online Network.**

"Some online retailers will be threatened by Amazon's move into other product categories" but being the best site for one product or service is a better and easier path for most retailers online.
**– Nicole Vanderbilt, Analyst, Jupiter Communications, Inc., New York**

"We are very close to a major competitive push by some very much larger companies. My expectation is that when those players come online, we'll see redistribution of market share."
**– Jonathan Cohen, First Vice President and Chief Internet Strategist for Merrill Lynch & Co.**

"They work hard to keep their customers. They have the advantage that they work on the Net all the time, whereas their competitors are bricks-and-mortar stores that are still trying to figure the Net

out. And their market is now only a few hundred million dollars less than Barnes & Noble's – how insulting is that? That makes them the story everybody loves to tell, but they live up to it by being quick to respond to changes."
**– Melissa Bane, Senior Analyst, Yankee Group, May 1998**

# BIBLIOGRAPHY

Anonymous (1998) "Amazon.com: the wild world of e-commerce," *Business Week*, December 14.

Romenesko, James (1997) "Amazon.com's success has come faster than founder expected," *Knight-Ridder/Tribune Business News*, July 21.

Meyer, Michael (1998) "Going shopping.com," *Newsweek*, August 17.

Hazleton, Lesley (1998) "Jeff Bezos: how he built a billion-dollar net worth before his company even turned a profit," *Success*, July.

Hazleton, Lesley (1998) "Jeff Bezos's Secret of Success," *Finance Week*, September 15.

Wolff, Michael (1998) "Merge and converge" *The Industry Standard*, December 4. See http://www.thestandard.net/articles/display/

Segaller, Stephen (1998) *Nerds: A Brief History of the Internet*, Oregon Public Broadcasting.

Anders, George (1998) "On-Line: Amazon.com purchases signal wider ambitions," *Wall Street Journal*, August 5.

Bombrun, Charles J. (1996) *Reputation: Realizing Value from the Corporate Image*, Harvard Business School Press.

Reed, Alastair (1998) "Seattle's Amazon could threaten booming U.K. booksellers," *Campaign*, August 7.

## One

# LIVE AND BREATHE E-COMMERCE

"Anytime there is change, there is opportunity."
**– Jack Welch, CEO, General Electric**

To understand the scale of Amazon.com's achievement you need to understand the basics of e-commerce. This chapter outlines some best e-business practice, principles which have contributed significantly to Bezos' phenomenal success. These are not unique to Amazon.com, of course, but for the budding entrepreneur or for anyone who wants to understand the secrets of Amazon.com's formula, it may be useful to have them all in one place.

Money can be made on the Web by those who start now. Revenues in 1997 amounted to $10.7 billion, a 3500 percent increase over the figure for 1995, according to International Data Corporation, a Framingham, Massachusetts-based media research firm. For 1998, e-commerce brought in $43 billion. By 2003, Forrester Research Inc. projects it will balloon to $1.3 trillion. In the US alone, by the year 2006, e-commerce may represent up to 40 percent of all business.

There are from 50 million to 100 million sites on the Web, but there is still room for more – for both business-to-business ventures and business-to-consumer operations based on economic models that couldn't work anywhere else, like in the real world (e.g. Amazon.com).

Of the sites on the Web, however, those that will succeed will be managed by people who understand e-commerce, individuals like Jeff Bezos and his management team. It is Bezos' understanding of the Web and Web users that has made his cyberstore one of the most popular sites on the Web.

# UNDERSTAND E-COMMERCE: WHAT'S ON THE WEB, WHAT ISN'T THERE

There are three kinds of e-commerce. The first is made up solely of advertisements and other information about a firm's products or services on its Web site. The purpose is to reach new markets and grow nationally or, better still, globally. The second is in the form of a brochure or catalog online to market the firm's products more cheaply. The third is actually to run a business based on what the Web can do, like Amazon.com, which is able, due to the Web, to market a wider selection of products than could be found in any brick-and-mortar store; offer personalized service to customers, including alerting them to new products they might want to buy based on past purchases; and entertain them sufficiently to make them want to come back.

"The exciting reality is that e-commerce is in its infancy. It is today where the Wright brothers were in aviation. The Web is still an infant technology."

**Jeff Bezos**

Of the millions of sites on the Web, the majority don't fall into any of these categories, even the first. These sites serve only to give the creator of the site a presence on the Web. Of the professional services sites, their intent is frequently the first of the three, but often these sites consist of no more copy than could be found on a business card or in a small brochure, with a hotlink added to allow visitors to e-mail the sites' creators.

A long harangue about a firm's services isn't any better as the basis for a Web site. The ideal site offers information about its products or services in an exciting, interactive, useful fashion.

## KNOW WHAT THE MEDIUM DEMANDS

I have a colleague who acknowledges the potential of the Web but hasn't the patience to surf it – and with cause. Unless you know exactly where you are going, surfing the Web for information or to make a purchase often means visits to numerous boring or pathetic sites. Many individuals who put them up haven't put themselves in the shoes of site visitors and made it as easy as possible for them to find out what they're promoting or selling, make a selection if it's a cyberstore, then order it, maybe with a single click, via e-mail, and/or an 800-number.

Visitors to a Web site are like visitors to a store who are "just looking." The editorial content (equivalent to displays in a store) should draw them in and keep them there until they make a selection. After all, there are no sales clerks to offer to help in order to encourage an extended visit until the shopper discovers something to purchase or bookmarks the site for another visit. With a mouse, it takes only a few seconds for a user to make a decision to stay or move on.

A mouse is comparable to a TV remote, with the user's finger poised to click to go elsewhere. If a site doesn't interest, the user will click out, never to return; if the content catches a prospective buyer's interest, then the mouse will be clicked to find more.

Even a site built solely to advertise an organization's existence and services must give visitors reason to come and learn more, which is why consulting and other professional service firms include white papers offering free management advice and why associations provide updated research, and various businesses continually update their sites with information on how best to use their products. Businesses that use their sites to supplement traditional distribution channels will offer information about their products, industry, and related subjects. Visitors can download full product descriptions, pricing, and purchase information, even full catalogs.

## CHANGE YOUR PAGES REGULARLY

A Web page devoted to e-commerce doesn't have to change daily as Internet enthusiasts expect an online newsletter to change, but contents should be freshened on a regular basis. Those who visit a site and bookmark it in order to return will expect revisions upon their return. Otherwise, they won't return again.

If you want to get return visitors to your site, at least one item on your site must change frequently – ideally daily but at least weekly to ensure that it is different each time a user visits. It can be as simple as a daily aphorism or coverage of a current industry development, or a new tool or technique for product users. Contests or giveaways will also draw visitors again and again to a site. Amazon.com came up with lots of contests itself, giving visitors the opportunity to pen poems, help finish final chapters, name books by best-selling authors, or even complete a *Doonesbury* cartoon strip.

As you plan or storyboard your site, you should think about those elements that could lend themselves to quick and simple change. Let's say that you plan to set up a small store on the Web. Besides the catalog, you might want to include information about your product – like how best to make a selection, when to use the item, or maintenance and repair. You may want to plan to update these customer alerts but you may also want to provide an archive so previous past alerts are still available to visitors.

Consider the value of graphics, too. While the site is being designed, choose several color schemes. Consequently, besides content changes, you can change the background color of the site every couple of weeks. Likewise, illustrations on the site. Changing an image every time the page is changed will make the page look fresh to past visitors.

Sites that promise to be updated by a certain date should be sure to keep that promise. If they don't, return visitors who find the same contents on the site won't come again. Even if they are only a day or two behind schedule, they will have disenchanted those who came on the date when they expected the revisions and found "the same old stuff."

I admit to being a horoscope nut. I love to read those not only for my sign but my friends' signs. There are a few sites to which I go regularly. Recently, I learned about a site that offered monthly forecasts. It was almost the end of the month, so I had to satisfy my interest with projections for the month I was in. But I looked forward to the first of the month when I would get predictions for the next 30 days. When I arrived, I found the site hadn't been changed. Nor had it been changed the following day. I expect it's been changed by now, but it's no longer bookmarked by me and I doubt I could find it again. Nor do I care to do so.

While I personally don't like hitting a site and being welcomed by name, most users enjoy this personalization. So investment in software that allows this capability is generally worthwhile. Before the visitor leaves, you can ask for his or her name, e-mail address, and other information, including product interests and concerns, via a customer survey. Next time the visitor comes to your site, with this software, he or she will be greeted by name and told, "We noticed you were concerned about … We are now offering a new, improved … If you're interested, click here for more information."

At the very least, consider how you can get the name and e-mail address of any visitors to your site.

## FOLLOW UP WITH VISITORS

Most well-designed sites offer some reason for visitors to the sites to leave their e-mail addresses. This way those who put up the sites have a means for pursuing business later, even if it is with traditional direct mail or telemarketing. Unfortunately, however, a lot of the addresses are incorrectly typed – sometimes as many as half. Consequently, besides asking for e-mail addresses, sites that don't want to lose touch with visitors should ask as well for telephone numbers or addresses. Snail mail can be used if the e-mail address doesn't work.

## STAY AHEAD OF WEB TECHNOLOGY

As you will see in Chapter 8, if you do business on the Web, you are doing business in one of the fastest changing, most complex industries. Given the operating timeframe on the Web and the impact that both cyberbuzz and ever-competing technologies can have, it is tough enough to maintain current market share – let alone grow that share. But commitment to e-commerce demands that an entrepreneur stay one step ahead of the technology curve.

If an entrepreneur can, he or she should buy the technology needed, Bezos has told reporters. Such technology wasn't available when Amazon.com was launched and consequently Bezos and his initial staff of three created their own software. The site's 1-Click™ ordering system is proprietary to the firm, too. Since its launch in 1995, Amazon.com has made numerous technological additions and adaptations to give prospective customers reason to visit and to keep current customers satisfied with service from the cyberstore.

## OFFER ONLINE ORDERING CAPABILITY

Once Web users were reluctant to order online. This reluctance is slowly disappearing. With this disappearance is an increase in online ordering capability. Most online systems work similarly to Amazon.com, in which users provide credit card information to establish an account and thereafter the information is accessed when the user orders again. For those still reluctant to send credit card information over the Web, most sites that offer online ordering give users the option of ordering as well by fax or telephone.

# KNOW ABOUT YOUR CUSTOMERS

It shouldn't be necessary to say, but too often we forget to consider for whom our site was created. If a site is to be useful to a visitor, you need to have a clear picture of who that visitor will be. You need to understand the targeted market and, equally important, what kind of value proposition you can offer them and the means by which you will alert them to your site. The nature of the product or service offered will determine your targeted audience and then your strategy to bring them to your destination.

There is some general information we know about the Internet population. At present, more than half are male, with most users aged 20–24 or 35–45. Most Internet enthusiasts are highly educated, with technical or professional, or educational careers; younger visitors make from $21,000 to $25,000, older visitors from $40,000 to $45,000. These demographics may change as Web usage grows and more older individuals join the Internet population.

Jeff Bezos did careful research to determine which kind of products would sell well on the Web. The kinds of products fall into four categories:

1   Products that would appeal to Internet users. So you could sell keyboards or mouse pads, or computer software. Within this category should be added online newsletters and magazines (referred to as e-zines) that can be read either on screen or downloaded and read like traditional publications.

2   A hard-to-find or unique product only available through
the Web. These are products that usually
have a market too small to be reached
profitably via a category store.
Online is even more cost effective
than direct mail or via display
for sale at trade shows or industry meetings where there
are product sales.

3   Price-driven products.
Browsers know already what
they want. If it is more convenient to purchase it on the
Web, then they will go to
your site to buy it. But they
usually expect to pay less than
they would at a brick-and-mortar store to make up for cost of
postage and delivery costs.

> "I think ideas
> are easy. It's
> execution that's
> hard. If you and I were
> to sit here for an hour
> and scribble on this chalk
> board on the wall, we
> could come up with a
> hundred good ideas. The
> hard part is making them
> work, and there are
> several key
> components in
> that."
> **Jeff Bezos**

4   A product or service targeted specifically to those individuals who frequent the
net: technically savvy, information-seeking individuals who
visit the net as much for business purposes as for entertainment.

Bezos' initial plan was designed around selling products that
fit into the third and fourth categories. As he has worked to get
people to his site, he has moved beyond the initial list to provide other reasons, like his recent decision to run auctions at
his site and, prior to that, his decision to help purchasers on
the Web compare prices of items.

# SUCCESSFUL SITES

Interested in doing business on the Web? If you already have a site, here are some questions to ask yourself. The more questions you can answer "yes," the more likely you will be successful at e-commerce.

◆ Is my site registered with search engines like Lycos, AltaVista, HotBot, Excite, InfoSeek, DogPile, Jeeves, and the like?

◆ Is the material on my site always new or updated, and is the look always fresh?

◆ Do the pages contain reader-friendly content?

◆ Does it take only a second or two for visitors to the site to know the nature of my business?

◆ Are the navigation aids easy to follow?

◆ Is the site accessible by many browsers?

◆ Jeff Bezos talks about providing a "value proposition" to customers; in other words, cyberstores succeed that provide personalized service, information, and fun. Does your site offer this value-added?

◆ Does the site offer a means of communication with visitors (e.g. e-mail)?

◆ Does the site take advantage of the interaction available through the Web?

◆ Is the site used not only to provide information to customers but also to get information from customers?

◆ Does the site throughout have consistency in both graphics and content?

# PUT YOUR CATALOG ONLINE

Placing the entire product line on the Web can be a cost-effective way to market to Web users. The best online catalogs are those that are more than lists. Organized to reflect customer thinking, the catalog should include sufficient detail of each product to enable users to make purchase decisions. A cyberstore can even go one step further, as Amazon.com has done, and set up a search engine to locate products. Each title has its own page, with picture of the jacket or cover, or packaging, a description of the contents, and related information. Further, as Amazon.com has done, personalize the site so that purchase information is kept on customers and used to make recommendations when they return to the site.

## HOTLINK ON RELATED SITES

It pays to look at the Web to identify sites that are related to yours, then contact their Web masters to see if they will agree to your having a hotlink on their site. If these site managers are wise, they will be agreeable to adding a hotlink on their page in return for a hotlink on your site.

Why? Let's assume someone is interested in purchasing a humidor for a friend. Your site sells cigars and special blends of tobacco for pipes. Seeing the hotlink to your site, the purchaser might click to your site to see your cyberstore's offerings and then, on impulse, purchase a sample or sign up for that special offer you have to provide new blends every month, or request more information about your product. The impulse buy works the other way as well. Someone at your site purchasing a new tobacco blend might see the hotlink, click to the other cyberstore, and buy a humidor or new pipe, or other product sold there.

Lots of associations offer hotlinks to sites to help their membership do their work. You may want to consider those organizations with which you would want to be associated. Check their site. If they offer hotlinks, see if your site can be added.

You may also want to look into association affinity programs. Increasingly, associations are building relationships with product producers and service firms, contracting to promote specific ones in return for discounts to members. Often, these discounted items are provided via hotlinks on the association's Web sites. Again, look for those trade or professional associations that would be interested in your site's offering and see if you can work out a deal.

## LET PEOPLE KNOW YOUR ADDRESS

You can create an exciting, interactive, informative Web site, yet you will get fewer visitors than your work deserves if you don't promote your Web page aggressively and relentlessly. The need to bring traffic to Amazon.com is why Bezos continues to add products for sale at his cyberstore and to keep adding services as well; his goal is to give prospective buyers reason to visit the site and perhaps purchase a book or a video or audio cassette, or other product available at the site. It's also the reason behind agreements with various search engines and strategic alliances (see Chapter 10).

Promotion of a Web site takes two forms: offline and online. Offline, addresses can be placed on business cards and brochures – letterhead stationery, too. If a business produces a product, it should place its Web address on all product information.

The site suggests to potential customers that the firm is technologically advanced. The contents on the site can be written to answer frequently asked questions (FAQs) and to enable the organization to inform potential, new, and existing customers more about the firm. The site itself can also be an excellent place to gather information about customers and build a sense of community, which can contribute to customer retention.

Although your cyberstore is virtual, you will want to advertise in the real-time on radio and television, or whichever media your potential customers are likely to use. Site name can determine whether offline advertising is easy or not. Think of some of the more convoluted Web site names, then compare them to Amazon.com, named both for ease in promotion and brand enhancement, or other simple cyberstore names or Web sites, like Landsend.org or AMA.com, or photodisc.com. On TV, be sure that Web site names are displayed long enough for viewers to write them down correctly. On radio spots, they should be pronounceable.

Of course, you should be advertising on the Web as well. Banners are one form of advertisement there. Banners are small graphic buttons or images inviting users to click for more information. This approach is comparable to a direct mail campaign using the mailing list for the *New York Times*, *Chicago Tribune*, or *London Times*; a large percentage of readers won't be interested in the product or service being offered, but there will be some and they could be prospective customers. A Web alternative to these periodicals are the various search engines on the Web. Cost may be high for a banner ad, and negotiation may take time, but it is worth consideration. Since there are always new search engines, you may be able to get a good deal with a fledgling engine likely to appeal to your potential customers. If you are opening a cyberstore, this is one way of building name recognition, even if viewers of your banner don't come to your store.

Certainly you should list your Web site with every search engine available. Each search engine has a different purpose. For instance, Yahoo!'s purpose is very different from Alta Vista's, which is very different from Excite, which is very different from Go To. One of the earliest search engines was Yahoo! but it is more used by homebodies for personal searches than Hotbot or AltaVista, which are used more often by businesses for business-to-business searches. Popularity of search engines also rises and falls, and new search engines are forever coming on the Web, like www.dogpile and www.askjeeves, both of which allow surfers to seek sites by writing full sentences, making them more user-friendly.

## PROMOTE CYBERBUZZ ABOUT YOUR SITE

Jeff Bezos and Amazon.com excel in the use of press relations. As Bezos contracts with smaller sites to link with Amazon.com through its Associates Program, press releases are posted on appropriate Usenet newsgroups and search engines. Like lots of other companies, Amazon.com also has company information, including copies of each press release about a stage in the business' growth.

It's interesting to note that Amazon.com began promoting itself even before its launch, via discussion groups and other chat rooms. This is a valuable tip for entrepreneurs who want to get traffic flow to their site as quickly as possible: Amazon.com used cyberbuzz through discussion forums and chat groups to generate interest and get users going to the site. It's been said, "If you build it, they will come." Not so. A cyberstore, no matter how exciting or informative its contents, or how good its merchandise, or how large the price savings offered, won't succeed unless people know it's there.

## GETTING STARTED ON THE WEB

If you are to make money on the Web, you have to understand e-commerce like Jeff Bezos does. Which means you have to decide what you want to do on your Web site. Bezos chose to run a business on the Web, but existing businesses can expand their market share by using the Web as a new distribution chain. You can also use the site solely to get leads for phone followup.

Be clear about the logistics. If you plan to sell on the Web, you need to be sure of every detail, including the source of inventory, management of the editorial content on the site, packaging, and shipping. As you develop your plan, remember that, like Amazon.com, you don't have to maintain your own inventory – you can purchase from other suppliers. On the other hand, you should give serious consideration to having your site maintained by your own staff to ensure consistency of content and design and timely refreshment.

Provide suitable graphics. You want a site that looks good but also doesn't take forever to download. Web users aren't patient people, so most important information about the cyberstore should be the first content seen. Visit Amazon.com. Study it. Besides the fact that it opens quickly, isn't it clear that you are

# HELP PEOPLE FIND YOU

The key to financial success of a Web site is traffic. From my own work on Web sites, I know an organization can't promote its presence, offer customer service, charge advertisers, or make sales unless people visit the site. Bezos knows this; it's why he continues to provide reasons for past customers to visit and new Web users to check out the site.

Once you have designed your site and launched it, don't forget these inexpensive – sometimes free – ways to let potential users know that your site is open and its URL, or address:

◆ **E-Mail Ads.** A friend of mine runs a fan site and each time I receive an e-mail message from her I know it will include a message at the bottom with the address of the site. The message is courtesy of one of the many e-mail programs that allow users to create files of text that automatically append to the bottom of all e-mails. These messages are called "signature files," and you should use them in e-mail messages to new and current customers. If you already have a business, you do e-mail promotions, and the Web site is designed to expand it geographically or via an additional distribution channel, you can encourage traffic to your new site by including a brief ad, such as: "Visit our Web site at www.newsite.com to reduce purchase costs by another 15 percent." The secret to use of the signature file is to keep your message short – no more than two to four lines of text. Too long, and the recipient won't read it. Think of it as a postscript in a letter. Kept short, the recipient will read it and be more likely to remember the message.

◆ **Direct e-mail.** You don't want customers to come once. You want them to keep coming each time you have made improvements to the site, including new product offerings. If you already do e-mail promotions to customers, next time add a question asking if they would like to be notified of changes or updates to your Web site. If they say yes, create a mailing list that e-mails them each time you have made an improvement in your site or have another service or product for sale. Be discriminating in the use of this. Use this opportunity only when you truly have some new products available on the site or key issues addressed there. The e-mail message should serve the equivalent of a teaser on a number 10 letter as part of a direct mail campaign.

◆ **Post to online billboards.** There are about 16,000 newsgroups, which behave like bulletin boards. Each newsgroup is on a specific topic, from pet care to latest performances of former Tony award winners, to developments in e-commerce, to concerns of administrative assistants, to general management and business issues. Check out those in areas related to your business. Monitor the newsgroup or bulletin board for a few weeks to see how tolerant it is to posted ads from Web sites about themselves or their services or products. Or send an e-mail message asking if you could leave a message about your business. Some groups are violently opposed to such listings, and there are stories about businesses that have tried to use newsgroups to promote their operations only to be flamed by hate e-mail. But if the newsgroup appears to allow brief messages so long as the subject line is clear about the nature of the message, then post your message. Use as a subject line: "Great opportunity to save!" or "Info on new product distributor." The message itself should be clear: "I am CEO of Company X, and here's how you can reach us if you're interested in learning more about our product line."

◆ **List on search engines.** Not listing on all the search engines on the Web is equivalent to opening up a traditional business and not listing in the local Yellow Pages. Even if it means you will be among hundreds, if not thousands, listed in certain categories, you should put yourself on every search engine. After all, if you aren't listed, people won't find you at all. When you list, you will be asked for keywords to determine where your site should be listed. Complete your list, then test the keywords to be sure they take you among those with whom you should be listed. Be honest with Web users. You can alienate potential customers if you advertise on the search engine "albums of popular oldies," but only sell a few tapes from the '60s and otherwise sell current music. Since those who search the Web via search engines will click, check quickly the site, then move on unless they find what they want, besides delivering what you promise, here are four tips about managing the site itself to make someone using a search engine appreciate what you have developed:

◆ **Don't make a visitor wait** to download the site. Put aside those large photos. You can create interesting visual effects that don't take so long to download.

◆ **Include information** to help the Web user contact the company in real time, like its phone and fax number and address. This lends credibility to the company advertised on the Web as well as provides more traditional contact methods if it finds it can't reach the site by e-mail.

◆ **Update sites frequently.** Ideally, sites should be updated at least weekly. Admittedly this makes their maintenance labor intensive, but keeping a site fresh with new information is critical to getting return visitors.

◆ **Offer interaction.** There are two elements of the Web that set it apart from other forms of communication: It allows for timely reports *and* for interaction. One way to bring interaction to your site is to allow visitors to search a product database by keyword. Another interactive tool could be an online form for visitors to use to request company or product information, additional customer service or a customized e-mail newsletter.

at a cyberstore? Although the site's opening page is admittedly busy, it catches interest rather than turns off visitors.

Develop editorial content to fully utilize the medium. You want content that is exciting, interactive, and informative; that gives those on the Web a reason to revisit your site. Each time they come should represent another opportunity to make a sale.

Organize your catalog for quick access. You want navigational tools that enable a user to find what he or she wants quickly, click to get purchasing information, then put through an order.

Have a comprehensive and aggressive promotion plan. Bezos began by making future visitors to Amazon.com aware of the new cyberstore by encouraging discussion of his site at discussion forums and other chat rooms. The name itself was chosen to reflect the cyberstore's vision but it also served to draw Internet enthusiasts' attention to the virtual store. Within a year of its opening, agreements were made with almost all the major search engines. Subsequently, the site added banners on other sites. Finally, the organization initiated its Advantage program that allowed smaller sites to hotlink to Amazon.com in return for revenues derived from the linkage.

Keep the interest alive. Just as Jeff Bezos continues to do, successful cyberstores will keep adding new features, new reasons for people to drop by, look around, and buy. Contrary to what many first-timers on the Web think, getting a site up isn't the end of the development of the site; it's actually the beginning. Each day, you need to be thinking about a new way to bring visitors to the site. There's an economic reality about a cyberstore: You may get thousands, hundreds of thousands of hits or visits ultimately each day, but only a very small percentage of those visitors – sometimes less than one percent – will buy. Consequently, you must continually give reason for new visitors to check out the site and old visitors to return on the off chance that this time they will buy.

# BIBLIOGRAPHY

Slovan, Margie (1997) "Bound for the Internet," *Nation's Business*, March.

Seybold, Patricia B., with Marahak, Ronni T., *Customers.com*, Times Books, New York.

Jamison, Brian, Gold, Josh and Jamison, Warren, *Electronic Selling: 23 Steps to E-Selling*, McGraw-Hill, New York.

Holtz, Shel, *Public Relations on the Net: Winning Strategies to Inform and Influence the Media, the Investment Community, the Government, the Public, and More!* Amacom, New York.

de Jonge, Peter (1999) "Riding the wild, perilous waters of amazon.com" *New York Times Magazine*, March 14.

## Two

# FILL THE PLACE WITH ENTREPRENEURS

"The foremost distinguishing feature of effective managers seems to be their ability to recognize talent and to surround themselves with able colleagues."

**– Norman R. Augustine, President and CEO,**
*Augustine's Laws*

M uch has been written about the startup of Amazon.com; little has been written about its staffing. Consequently, the press stood up and took notice when a $100 million lawsuit was filed by Wal-Mart against Amazon.com in November 1998. Also defendants in the case were Kleiner, Perkins, Caulfield, Amazon's venture capitalist, and another Kleiner client, DrugStore.com, then seven months old. Amazon.com has recently purchased a minority interest in DrugStore.com.

The suit alleged that Amazon.com and the others had hired away Wal-Mart employees and former consultants to gain proprietary information about the retailer. A Wal-Mart spokesperson said that potential trade secrets could be lost in data warehousing, distribution, and merchandising systems, and "Retail Link," Wal-Mart's buyer decision support software.

In September 1997, Amazon had hired Richard Dalzell as its chief information officer. Thereafter, according to the Wal-Mart suit, Amazon.com had brought other IS employees to work for the firm in Seattle. The company denied the allegations.

## SEEK OUT TALENTED PEOPLE

Amazon.com responded that none of the Wal-Mart employees had non-compete contracts; Amazon had explicitly instructed its employees not to use or disclose any Wal-Mart trade secrets; and Wal-Mart and Amazon.com operations, software, and hardware were so different that there was no threat of lost trade secrets. Amazon.com's defense also included one other not-so-insignificant point: Wal-Mart's founder, Sam Walton, in his book *Made in America,* had bragged that throughout his career he would "nose around other people's stores searching for good talent." The story goes that this little detail was found by Bezos himself who, upon learning about the suit, ordered books about Wal-Mart, from Amazon.com of course.

Bezos said, "We aren't interested in anyone's trade secrets. But we are very interested in talented people." Which would appear to be what Bezos got. With Dalzell and former Wal-Mart employees on board, Amazon.com revenue over a nine-month period jumped to $357 million, from $82 million over a nine-month period the year before. Customer accounts increased five-fold, from 940,000 to nearly 4.5 million.

The press has heard no more about the case. But the incident raises a question about how Bezos will retain his top team members if those with e-commerce plans troll for Web experience. Certainly Bezos's organization would seem as much a target for raiders as brick-and-mortar retailers like Wal-Mart or other Web operations like barnesandnoble.com and Bol.com, or Web portals, like AOL. If you wish to build a Web-based organization, what can you offer that will recruit and retain the e-experience you need?

## RAISE THE TALENT LEVEL OF NEW RECRUITS

John Doerr of Kleiner, Perkins told Stephen Segaller, author of *Nerds: A Brief History of the Internet,* that Amazon had an outstanding person in Bezos, as founder and CEO, but that it needed a strong management team and that he, together with Bezos, had chosen each and every member carefully. But how can Bezos safeguard this rich resource of knowledge about e-commerce? He put together one associate at a time, reportedly over café latte at the Starbuck in a Barnes and Noble located near his apartment. Bezos has said his people are one key to the organization's success. One reporter – Chip Bayers – referred to Bezos's hiring style as "a Socratic test," in which candidates endured interviews not only with Bezos but other staff members. After Bezos interviewed a candidate, he would interview the other interviewers, drawing elaborate charts to reflect the individual's qualifications. If there was the slightest doubt, a candidate would be rejected. An individual who made it through the recruitment process told Bayers that each time someone was hired the recruitment bar was raised, thereby continually improving the overall quality of the staff.

## WHO MAKES UP BEZOS' TOP TEAM?

Richard Dalzell is chief information officer. Formerly the vice-president of information systems for Wal-Mart Stores, he was a key defendant for Amazon.com in the Wal-Mart case. George T. Aposporos is vice-president of business development. Before joining Amazon.com, he was founder and president of Digital Brands, a strategic consulting and interactive marketing firm, and as such placed Starbucks in the first campaign to use animated advertising on America Online. In charge of editorial content and design of the Web site is the former executive editor for technology at *PC Magazine,* Rick Ayre, vice president and executive editor at Amazon.com. Amazon.com's chief financial officer, Joy D. Covey, was vice president of business development and vice president of operations for the broadcast division of Avid Technology, a leader in the digital media industry, before coming to Amazon.com. In charge of supplier relationship and direct purchasing is Mary Engstrom Morouse, who came to Amazon.com from Symantec where she served as vice president of product marketing. Sheldon J. Kaphan is currently chief technology officer, but he was vice-president of research and development from October 1994 to March 1997 and, as such, was responsible for developing Amazon.com's software and maintaining the company Web site.

> A reporter noted that Bezos' executive staff is a "motley, though whip-smart, band of executives ranging from Microsoft refugees to liberal-arts majors and rock musicians."

John David Risher, senior vice president of product development, came to Amazon.com from Microsoft Investor, Microsoft Corporation's Web site for personal investment. Another former Microsoft manager is Joel R. Spiegel, vice president of engineering at Amazon.com. At Microsoft, Spiegel held several positions, including Windows 95 Multimedia development manager, Windows Multimedia group manager, and product unit manager for information retrieval. Like Dalzell, Amazon.com's chief logistics officer was previously at Wal-Mart, from which he retired as vice president of distribution.

## ONCE YOU HAVE THE BEST, GIVE THEM REASON TO STAY

Given his need to conserve cash for expansion, Bezos decided to give his employees – managers and employees – a piece of the action to keep them. Employees now number more than 1000, small for a brick-and-mortar retail chain but a huge jump from the three individuals who worked in Bezos's garage those first few days prior to Amazon.com's launch. Employees in his warehouse, as well as office staff and top team members, are all members of the firm's profit sharing program, although "goal sharing" might be a better term for the program since its worth is a measure of individuals' belief in Bezos' promise "to build a valuable and *lasting* company."

There is nothing new about profit sharing. In 19th century Europe, it wasn't unusual for an artisan to be paid a portion of the profits for his craftsmanship. Instead of an hourly rate, he got a share of the payment for the final work. When the owner of the shop retired, he often left a portion of the business to each artisan who worked for him. These were the first profit sharing plans – and possibly the first retirement plans, too.

By the early twentieth century, several US firms were providing profit-sharing programs based on corporate performance. In these pre-pension times, these plans meant more comfortable retirements, for some simply the possibility of retirement. But in the 1930s the situation changed. Legislation was passed which allowed employers to defer federal income taxes on profit shares that were contributed to a retirement trust. This caused workers to think of profit sharing as an entitlement, thereby lessening its impact on job performance. Social Security legislation passed around this time lessened the need for profit sharing at all.

Interest in these plans re-emerged in the 1970s as organizations looked for ways to improve motivation and reduce labor costs. As we enter the new millennium, company-specific hybrids are developing – programs like that at Au Bon Pain where store managers get to feel like franchisees by getting a cut of stores' profits over a negotiated time period or the Outback Steakhouse where managers can invest in their restaurants in return for 10 percent of cash flow (earnings before taxes, calculated monthly) over a five-year period. Since a single Outback Steakhouse can earn as much as $700,000 annually, an Outback manager can make as much as $70,000 in a year.

But a closer example, still, of the kind of solution that Bezos has implemented to keep his top team intact is one from Sam Walton himself. When Walton took Wal-Mart public in 1970, he offered managers a profit-sharing plan. His thinking was that happy managers would treat Wal-Mart employees well, and this would spill over to good customer service. But over the next 12 months, as he wrote in *Made in America,* Walton realized that satisfied, loyal employees were actually the secret to high profits. So in 1971, his company expanded its profit-sharing plan to include all employees, or "associates." The company's success meant that a truck driver who went to work for Walton and Wal-Mart in 1971 could make at least $700,000 in profit sharing. At Wal-Mart, these long-term benefits were supplemented by short-term incentives, and continue to be so.

Bezos would seem to have taken ideas from Au Bon Pain, Outback Steakhouse and Wal-Mart, and adapted them in ways that motivate his employees whilst maintaining a tight run ship. Like the Wal-Mart program, all of Amazon's associates are members, but Bezos' plan is long-term focused, with no short-term incentives. Employees get base pay at slightly less than market rates but they also get new-hire stock options at highly competitive levels upon joining the organization. Consequently, a warehouse employee hired for $20,000 in 1997 when the company went public had more than double that amount in paper gains only a year later. Thus, Bezos provides reason for his entrepreneurial team members to turn down raiders.

# ALIGN RECRUITMENT AND RETENTION TO CORPORATE CULTURE

From a dollars and sense view, Amazon.com is able to compete for the skill sets it needs to succeed, while maintaining a low operating margin. Funds that might have had to go to payroll can be put into marketing and other initiatives to finance expansion of the customer base, critical to the organization's success. Beyond that, this reward system is more likely to attract those most suitable to a startup than an established business. Amazon.com needs aggressive, out-of-the-box thinkers – highly committed managers and workers who are willing to invest in the long-term success of the online retail firm. And, whether intentionally or not, Bezos has put in place a screening device that will help select those who not only are willing to trade short-term returns for long-term potential but are believers in the success of Amazon.com. Otherwise, they would not agree to work for an upstart company where they have to pay a considerable part of the premium for medical coverage – thereby preserving dollars for market expansion – and which began in a drab 1960s-style four-story building without even a sign marking its presence.

In their book *Finding and Keeping Great Employees,* authors Dr Jim Harris and Dr Joan Brannick observe how firms that align

# ALIGNING RECRUITMENT AND RETENTION STRATEGIES WITH CORPORATE CULTURE

Jeff Bezos understands that Amazon.com can be only as good as its people, and to that end he has assembled top-notch talent throughout his organization. His staffing secrets extend beyond hiring the best, to hiring the best *for his organization* – an entrepreneurial business forging a place in mercantile history – then offering his employees ownership in the business to keep them. Specifically he:

◆ **Seeks talented people with related experience.** He knows the knowledge, skills, and abilities he needs to grow Amazon.com. Reviewing its strategic plan and likely challenges it will encounter, he has sought out individuals who will add to the team as a whole, not simply fill a specific position.

◆ **Involves others in the interview process.** As he listens to others, Bezos can undertake a 360 degree assessment, which allows him to avoid two problems many leaders, say the experts, commit in hiring:

  1  hiring people who mirror them in viewpoint or skill sets; and
  2  being unable to differentiate the sizzle of articulate interviewees from the steak of solid candidates with proven track records.

◆ **Recruits online for an online business.** While Bezos uses various recruitment channels, the most effective may be his own Web site with its call for "exceptionally talented, bright, and driven people who want to build a lasting franchise in this world-changing industry."

◆ **Builds a sense of community.** Work may be hard but hard work, interspersed with moments of fun, can be tolerable for employees when their boss shares both the hard work and the fun with them.

◆ **Gives his employees ownership in the company.** At a time when those with e-experience can write their own ticket, and Bezos has to invest most profits back into the business for expansion, he is able to pay his people less than marketplace salaries, yet keeps them by giving them two reasons for staying with the organization: the challenge of making the dream of e-commerce a reality and the financial rewards that come from ownership of a part of that dream.

recruitment and retention strategies with corporate culture are more successful in finding and keeping the right people. Drs Harris and Brannick call the strategy 'get real' and believe that this technique allows candidates to consider the positives and negatives of a job – which in Amazon's case would be the excitement of being in on the start of a major new form of business, with its innovative/risk taking climate, and stock options versus the noncompetitive pay and very long hours – and decide for themselves whether the company was an opportunity that they wanted to pursue.

## RECRUIT ONLINE FOR AN ONLINE BUSINESS

The employees who have been attracted to Amazon have been called "eclectic" by the business press – a "motley, but whip-smart band." They have varied backgrounds – from BScs in computer sciences to BAs in liberal arts. But what they have in common, Bezos has said, is a belief that together they are making a major change in the world. Potential employees may show up at the company's headquarters in Seattle or send snail mail, but most enquiries come from online, through the site's own recruitment program. On the Amazon.com site can be found this employment ad: "As a pioneer in this new marketplace, we're building an important and lasting company – and making history as we do it. But we don't stop at providing products and information that inspire, educate, and entertain our millions of customers – we also offer a work environment full of exceptionally talented, bright, and driven people ... If you'd like to work with us to build a lasting franchise in this world-changing industry (and have a great time doing it), *let us know.*" In case you still aren't sold, the announcement adds, "... since this is very possibly the worst five-year period in history not to have equity ownership, you should know that compensation for all of our openings includes stock options."

Who would turn down that kind of offer?

## PROMOTE A SENSE OF COMMUNITY

The Container Store is an 18-chain store that sells storage and organization products. Whereas it shares with Amazon.com a customer-centric culture, The Container Store pays employees above industry average to ensure continued high levels of personalized service and employee retention rates. Amazon.com pays less for the same dedication because of its equity program *and,* as important, the *esprit de corps* built around a shared belief in Amazon. In *Finding and Keeping Great Employees,* Bill Silberman, a long-time compensation and benefits executive, refers to the "intangible benefits of membership." "Pride in organizational brand and in being part of something important, and team spirit," he says, "can be more important than the tangible benefits of pay and benefits." Not that money isn't important, because it is, but money incentives are only a part of retention strategies for most world-class organizations. Creative organizations tie superior employees to the organization through corporate culture and purpose.

## DEMAND EMPLOYEES WORK LONG, HARD AND SMART

These intangibles have brought many of its employees to Amazon.com and will keep them there, despite the hard and grueling work. Bezos is said to continually raise the performance bar for managers, demanding higher and higher goals be met, which is accepted practice because Bezos makes similar demands on himself.

Like workers at Home Depot, where employees are expected to "bleed orange," referring to the color of the aprons they wear, Amazon.com staff are expected to work hard, long *and* smart for its success. Note the emphasis on "smart." It's as important to Bezos that his people work "smart" as that they work hard. Which is very much like Bill Gates' attitude. People who have worked for Gates say that you can be assured of his attention when you out-think him on an issue.

Bernie Marcus, Depot's chairman, has said: "The dedication we have to our customers is not a paper dedication … we must really live for the customers. From a value standpoint, from a quality standpoint, from a pricing standpoint, from a feeling that someone is treating them like a human being – that's really our goal. If we continue to do that, I don't see any limit to where The Home Depot can go."

# HOW TO BUILD A SENSE OF TEAM

If you want to build a sense of teamwork among your employees, you want your employees to:

◆ **Look at their responsibilities** in terms of the organization's survival. When managers and employees understand the impact they can have on the bigger picture, they are more motivated to pull together for the benefit of the organization.

◆ **Know and believe** in the short-term, medium-term, and long-term goals. When employees understand and are committed to the organization's mission and the strategic and tactical plans to achieve it, they appreciate their own importance to the company – the relationship between their responsibilities and the survival of the company as a whole – and they are willing to put in grueling hours to make the plans a reality.

◆ **Share responsibility.** Teamwork comes from shared responsibilities not only in doing the work but in making the decisions about what work is to be done. Having others support them, and recognize their role, is to support others too. Work is organized to make the most of each associate's contribution to the organization, bringing associates together so one can help another. Over time, employees learn the return from reliance on each other.

◆ **Acknowledge each other's accomplishments.** When staff can see the results of their efforts, they are encouraged to greater efforts.

◆ **Encouragement to use initiative.** Managers hold problem solving meetings or otherwise utilize the knowledge of staff members as they identify problems, prioritize them, and develop action plans to eliminate them.

◆ **Develop a common language** to foster cohesion and commitment. The words aren't important; it's the sharing that brings people together.

◆ **Have a team identity.** It's not that managers who are good at creating a sense of teamwork have all their workers running around with T-shirts with corporate logos on them, but they do look for rites and ceremonies that will draw the group together. In Bezos's case, that staff have no dress code – and employees run about bare-footed with torn jeans, or nose rings – may be that common identity.

◆ **Have inside jokes.** Good humor can relieve tension, particularly in a startup firm experiencing the tremendous stress from growth.

◆ **Share corporate histories.** No question, the story of Bezos's founding of Amazon.com will go down in corporate lore. In each telling, the story will probably get more audacious, but it will link each new hire to the next hire, as it already has done.

# KEEP EMPLOYEE ATTENTION ON THE RIGHT STUFF

Bezos is said to meet with his Seattle-based employees every third month to focus their attention toward values like customer service and increased productivity – and away from value of their stock portfolios. He worries that the ups of the stock market could make his people too self-confident and the downs of the marketplace too downcast. He told *BusinessWeek* that he tells his people, "Think about how you can create real value five years from now because we can actually affect the stock price five years from now, whereas none of us has any control over what the stock price is tomorrow."

In people management, location makes no difference in building an entrepreneurial team. Success stems from decentralized management and decision making, entrepreneurial innovation and risk taking, and high levels of employee commitment and enthusiasm.

# WOULD YOU TRUST YOUR MONEY TO THESE COMPUTER JOCKS?

An organization's success is the product of its people, their knowledge, and previous experience. Amazon.com is a community of talented individuals but, inevitably, investor attention focuses on its key decision makers:

◆ **Jeffrey P. Bezos.** According to Amazon.com, Bezos "has been interested in anything that can be revolutionized by computers." A graduate of Princeton University, where he received his degree in electrical engineering and computer science, he founded Amazon.com, Inc. in 1994. Prior to that, he helped manage more than $250 billion in assets for Bankers Trust. He also helped "build one of the most technically sophisticated quantitative hedge funds on Wall Street for D. E. Shaw & Co."

◆ **George T. Aposporos.** Before he joined Amazon.com in 1997 as vice-president of business development, Aposporos was president of Digital Brands, a strategic consulting and interactive marketing firm. To found the company, he left I.C.E., a Toronto-based multimedia developer and corporate communications firm where he was a vice-president and, as such, played a major role in its development of interactive television and Internet capabilities. Prior to his association with I.C.E. he was an independent producer in a variety of media, from TV to video, to CD-ROMs.

◆ **Rick Ayre.** Responsible for the editorial content and design of the Web site, Ayre is executive editor and a vice president at Amazon.com. He came to Amazon.com from *PC Magazine,* where he was executive editor for technology. While at the Ziff-Davis operation, he also ran *PC Magazine's* online services, including the *PC Magazine* Online Web site and PC MagNet, part of ZD Net on CompuServe. During his five years with the magazine, he was also the magazine's executive editor for software and, as technical director for software in PC Magazine Labs, supervised software product testing. Before his association with *PC Magazine,* he was chief of information resources at the Highland Drive VAMC, a Pittsburgh-based hospital. His technology career started while a Ph.D. candidate in psychiatric epidemiology at the University of Pittsburgh, where he learned to program in Fortran to manipulate data on an early DEC system.

◆ **Joy D. Covey.** Covey has been chief financial officer and vice president of finance and administration at Amazon.com since 1996. Besides her responsibility for financial and management systems and reporting, she manages planning and analysis, legal, administrative, investor relations, and human resources management. Before Amazon.com, she was vice-president of business development and vice president of operations for the broadcast division of Avid Technology. She joined the company following its merger in 1995 with Digidesign, where she was chief financial officer. While there, the company achieved more than 50 percent annual growth and built a strong position in the digital audio production systems market. Before Digidesign, Covey was a mergers and acquisitions associate at Wasserstein Perell & Co., an investment bank. She is a graduate of California State University where she got a BS in business administration, *summa cum laude*; she has both a JD and an MBA from Harvard.

◆ **Richard L. Dalzell.** Before coming to work for Amazon.com in 1997, as chief information officer with responsibility for its information systems, Dalzell was vice-president of information systems for Wal-Mart Stores, in charge of all its merchandising and logistics systems. Prior to joining Wal-Mart in 1990, he was business development manager for E-Systems and, before that, a teleprocessing officer in the U.S. Army.

◆ **Mary Engstrom Morouse.** Morouse joined Amazon in 1997 as vice president of publisher affairs and was appointed vice president of merchandising a year later. Before Amazon.com, Morouse was at Symantec where she was general manager of the security business unit and vice president of product marketing. While there, she played a major role in development, manufacture, distribution, and marketing of Symantec's line of antivirus and security products, including the Norton AntiVirus line. From 1989–1994, she was at Microsoft Corporation, where she held positions as group product manager for Microsoft Access, group product manager for Microsoft Project, and director of marketing in strategic relations.

◆ **Sheldon J. Kaphan.** Vice-president and chief technology officer since 1997, Kaphan was in at the firm's founding. As vice-president of research and development for the company from 1994 to 1997, he was responsible for developing Amazon.com's core software and maintenance of its site on the Web. Prior to his association with Amazon.com, he held senior engineering positions at Kaleida Labs, Frox, and Lucid.

◆ **John David Risher.** Risher came to Amazon.com as vice president of product development in February 1997, responsible for developing new products and services; before the year was up he was promoted to senior vice president of product development, with overall responsibility for product development, marketing, editorial, and content licensing. Before Amazon.com, Risher founded and was product unit manager for Microsoft Investor, Microsoft Corporation's Web site for personal investment. He was a member of the Microsoft Access product team before that, holding a variety of marketing and project management positions.

As Microsoft Access team manager, he managed all aspects of the product management team including design, development, branding, advertising, and customer research to produce Microsoft Access 95. Before joining Microsoft, he was an associate at the LEK Partnership, a management consulting firm.

◆ **Joel R. Spiegel.** Responsible for all Web site software, Spiegel joined Amazon.com in 1997 as vice-president of engineering. Like many other Amazon.com top team members, Spiegel was with Microsoft Corporation before coming to Amazon.com, holding positions as Windows 95 Multimedia development manager, Windows Multimedia group manager, and product unit manager for information retrieval. Before Microsoft, he was with Apple Computer, with various responsibilities, including new product development in the Apple Business systems Division. Prior to Apple, he held software product development positions at a number of other firms, including Hewlett-Packard and VisiCorp.

◆ **Jimmy Wright.** Latest addition to the top management team at Amazon.com, Wright came to the organization in 1998 as vice president and chief logistics officer, with responsibility for all global supply chain activities. He brought to the company more than 26 years experience in logistics management, including 12 years with Wal-Mart Stores. He joined Wal-Mart in 1985 and was vice president of distribution from 1990 until his retirement in 1998. A graduate of the University of Texas, where he received a BBA in personnel management, he began his career at the Fina Oil and Chemical Company, where he held a variety of positions, including general manager of distribution.

# BE PART OF THE COMMUNITY

At Amazon.com, the last – a sense of community – is a product as much due to Bezos's style of management as compensation programs he has put in place. Bezos does more than "talk the talk." He walks the talk. He is a part of the community that is Amazon.com not only by his dress-down appearance but his willingness to work as hard as everyone else, and – maybe even more important – play as hard as others during breaks. Fun isn't a luxury, even at work, where it can create team spirit that can sustain high performance. David Thielen, author of *The 12 Secrets of Microsoft,* points out that staff games of Nerf ball may not seem like a good use of employee time, but Nerf ball wars can cement a group. "The fact that this can be done at work is itself critically important," he wrote. "It tells the employees that the company is supportive of them enjoying themselves in the workplace. And that as long as the job is getting done, that's all that matters."

Bezos has been seen by the press, joining with his staff in a game called "broomball" by Amazonians – think hockey with a broom – or to joke, yuking it up with his staff with an explosive laugh that is said to be audible throughout the four-story building. This is as important as selection, direction, evaluation, and reward systems in an organization.

In the early years of Corporate Resource Development, an Atlanta-based sales and marketing services company, CEO and founder Max Carey needed a way to inspire his organization. His way to inspire his troops mirrors Bezos'. Carey went out and bought a siren, complete with megaphone and ambulance sound effects. After making a phone sales pitch, he would blow the horn if he had been able to get past gatekeepers and reach the CEO. If a check came in from a client, the siren blared. People would come out of their offices to hear their co-workers brag about their achievements. It built a team.

Bezos has built a team.

# BIBLIOGRAPHY

Anonymous (1998) "Amazon.com: the wild world of e-commerce," *BusinessWeek*, December 14.

Barner Robert W., (1994) *Crossing the Minefield: Tactics for Overcoming Today's Toughest Management Challenges* Amacom, New York.

Anonymous (1998) "Employee raiding cases hard to prosecute," *Computerworld*, October 26.

Harris, Jim and Brannick, Joan (1999) *Finding and Keeping Great Employees*, Amacom, New York.

Berry, Leonard L. Seiders, Kahleen and Gresham, Larry G. (1997) "For Love and Money: The Common Traits of Successful Retailers" *Organizational Dynamics*, Autumn, American Management Association.

Bayers, Chip (1999) "The inner Bezos" *Wired*, March.

Walton, Sam, with Huey, John (1993) *Made in America*, Bantam Books.

Thielen, David (1999) *The 12 Simple Secrets of Microsoft: How to Think and Act Like a Microsoft Manager & Take Your Company to the Top*, McGraw-Hill, New York.

## Three

# FOCUS

"A man without a goal is like a ship without a rudder."

On April 4, 1999, members of the business press received a press release via e-mail announcing the hostile takeover of Amazon.com by a small book publisher/Web bookstore. The press release came from the publisher's management.

As a member of the business press, I received a copy. In the final stages of writing this book, I admit to a sense of shock – and yes, frustration – as I realized that the acquisition would demand added chapters to this book. The story was a hoax, an April Fool's Day joke that misfired because of an e-mail foul-up, but for a few minutes it seemed believable in light of the many other developments over the last three years in what Bezos has called the "investing phase" of his cyberstore. Even as I work on this chapter which wryly addresses "focus" and "clarity of purpose," there is a radio announcement suggesting I visit Amazon.com to buy via auction a Hummel or beanie collectible.

And it is only one of several new developments at Amazon.com. This spring the organization added a fourth distribution facility, this one in Coffeyville, Kansas, to reduce shipping times to key markets in the midwest and southeast US. The existing 460,000 square foot facility will be expanded to more than 750,000 square feet before the year 2000, making it the largest Amazon.com distribution facility to date. Its recent purchase of Accept.com and Alexa Resources Inc. will put it further ahead in Web technology. Its purchase of Exchange.com means that it will have greater access to difficult-to-find books. The latest purchase – 35 percent of HomeGrocer.com – will give another link on the Web site for visitors.

So Amazon.com, since its launch, has gone from offering simply books, to selling music and videos. It has added various e-commerce services and has made strategic investments in various Web sites, including Pets.com, Drugstore.com, and now HomeGrocer.com. Yes, Amazon.com has gone from the "world's largest bookstore" to a destination site with the "world's largest selection," with links to numerous other sites where visitors can do comparison shopping, hotlinks to places where I can purchase prescription medicines, off-shelf medicines, groceries, and pull-toys for my dog. I can even bid for some object I never thought I wanted, until I saw it advertised at the site.

## MAINTAIN THE VISION

On the surface, it would seem that the vision behind Amazon.com has changed. Not so. If anything, the vision has been expanded beyond creation of a successful bookstore, to creation of a successful cyberstore with the world's largest selection. What Amazon.com has achieved, as reported in the business sections of our newspapers, is a reflection of the competitiveness on the Web in general and the moves of brick-and-mortar and cyberstores to compete directly with Amazon.com. Most importantly, by establishing a new economic model, Amazon has fulfilled one of its primary goals – to change the way business is conducted. In describing the decision to establish a fourth distribution center Amazon.com's chief logistics officer, Jimmy Wright, emphasizes the strategic focus of

**"Shoptainment" may be the value proposition for Amazon.com.**

Amazon.com: "Everything we do at Amazon.com is designed to continually enhance the customer experience." While Bezos and his team offer assurances about the eventual profitability of the organization, the business plan calls for heavy investment in the long-term – "ten-plus" years.

## FOCUS ON CORPORATE VALUE STREAMS

Corporate plans, when well made, play up what is called "strategic value streams;" that is, the unique qualities of the organization to move faster or better than its competitors. At Wal-Mart, it is the logistics system that enables the company to get the right goods to the stores at the right time at least cost. Cross-docking, which is the means by which goods are received and then sent on to different Wal-Mart stores, enables the company to buy and then distribute to stores to sell at discount. For Amazon.com, it is logistics – like speedy and secure delivery of orders – and, equally important, the customer value adding proposition so evident on a visit to the Web site. All strategic decisions made by Amazon.com's management would seem to be aimed at sustaining these two corporate strengths.

Beyond that, the decisions are a reflection of the sensitivity of the management team – in particular Jeff Bezos – to developments on the Web, and the interests and needs of the ever-increasing numbers of individuals going on the Web. Such sensitivity has been compared to radar. But growth on the Web has been so tremendous that there would seem to be numerous blips on the radar screen. And management at Amazon.com has had to make tough decisions about which blips to respond to.

# LAY FOUNDATIONS FOR THE FUTURE

If an organization is to achieve its longer-term goals, it needs to engage in the strategic planning process, defining those goals and direction for the future. The process demands:

◆ **Clarity about your purpose.** Whether an organization is on the Web or made from bricks and mortar, its leader must first define the nature of the business. In short, the CEO and top management team needs to answer the simple question, "Why are we here?"

◆ **Know where you are going.** After all, you can't get there unless you have some idea where you want to be five or ten years from now. Ideally, the long-term viewpoint should cascade down as short-term plans are made for the business.

◆ **Ask where are you now.** Most established businesses do such analysis of their market and strengths and weaknesses. But even relatively young businesses should ask themselves about strengths, weaknesses, opportunities, and challenges. A key point in reviewing challenges is to remember that they can be opportunities if viewed from a different perspective.

◆ **Practise strategic planning triage.** The group as a whole should identify the three most important areas of the business in which to excel to ensure overall corporate success.

◆ **Develop core outcomes.** Just as you have identified the mission and nature of the business, and long-term objectives, you have to identify short-term or nearer-term goals for the business (usually over a 12-month period) consistent with the purpose and CEO vision for the company.

◆ **Develop strategies for each outcome.** Strategies are different from tactics, which is the last step. Tactics are the step-by-step actions to be taken to achieve each strategy. Strategies are broader game plans for achieving each of the three outcomes identified. In Amazon.com's case, those outcomes were likely "shoptainment," "innovation," and "delivery."

◆ **Develop tactics.** These are the specific, measurable action plans – including the name of the person to be held responsible – tied to the strategies.

# HAVE A CLEAR SENSE OF PURPOSE

When an organization has so many directions in which it can proceed, it helps if management has a clear sense of the purpose of the organization. Too often, entrepreneurs see the purpose as the bottom line – sales volume or net profit, or some other numerical goal. These are of course critical, but during start-up and subsequent growth, financial objectives may not be enough to encourage extraordinary performance. The strategic focus should go beyond products or services – and the dollars earned from them – to aspirations to change the way the world operates. At Giro Sport Design, management and employees are proud to include in the helmets they sell, letters from grateful cyclists who describe how the Giro helmets have saved their lives. These notes are part of Giro's goal to make life safer and more satisfying. At Group Publishing, employees can point with pride to their founder, Thom Schulz, who saw a need for dynamic teaching materials for Sunday school and church education. The organization's goal is to be successful so it can provide literature that will catch the attention of young people raised on MTV. At Amazon.com, there is a sense of destiny beyond the organization's eventual profitability. In Amazonians' view, the cyberstore will change the world of retail, creating a blueprint for future e-tailers. It is a purpose that prompts employees at the Seattle firm to work hard and long hours. And from a business perspective, it sustains motivation. Employees don't need ask, "Why are we doing this?" and there isn't the usual problem of burnout because everyone at Amazon.com seems to be caught up in Bezos' dream.

## DEFINE YOUR OWN OPPORTUNITIES

It is Jeff Bezos' dream that keeps the company focused. It is also this dream, coupled with access to information about its customers, that enables the organization to determine, if not actually define, its opportunities rather than be driven by competitive pressures. While Bezos would seem to be moving from one kind of business on the Web to another, to still another, truth is that his purpose continues to be the same – to draw as many visitors to his Web site as possible to sell products and services appropriate for purchase on the Web. To do this he has had to:

◆ Identify existing cyberstores that already sell suitable products for his demographics and then link with them

◆ Identify most frequently trafficked sites and create partnerships (through acquisition, joint venture, or agreement) or emulate these sites.

Consider the kinds of products now available via Amazon.com. Had we had the list of 20 items that Bezos reportedly developed prior to launching Amazon.com, we know we would find books and videos and CDs and certainly computer software and hardware but there might also have been pharmaceuticals, pet supplies, maybe even groceries. If eBay brings considerable traffic to its site, then auctions would seem logical as well for Amazon.com even though such a move has meant the addition of another major competitor, this one with Web experience.

Management at fledgling firms will tend to seize opportunities since these will drive short-term growth. But longer-term growth is dependent on the organization's ability to stay focused on the business it wants to be in. And, despite all the new bells and whistles at Amazon.com, that business would appear to be e-tail. All the rest is the equivalent of a sideshow designed to bring in the customers. If you look at the site, it's clear that the company continues to focus on that thing that it does best and is committed to doing – which is to sell product on the Web. We're familiar with corporate mission statements. Walt Disney tells us it is in the business of "making people happy." 3M talks about "solving unsolved problems innovatively." Wal-Mart offers "to give ordinary folk the chance to buy the same thing as rich people." If I were to write Amazon.com's mission statement, it might be something like "to make the purchasing experience on the Web fun."

## PRACTISE TRIAGE

It would all seem so simple but it is far from it. Triage is most often thought in terms of medical practice, but a good CEO practises strategic triage. Jeff Bezos himself has used the term "triage" to point to the fact that he must often make tough decisions about how to move the organization for continuing growth and ultimate profitability. In the operating arena, triage is based on best survival rates of patients. In the corporate arena, it would seem based on growth drivers or corporate value stream. There are four primary drivers for growth:

◆ **Product focus.** The goal of organizations with a product focus is to make a product or line of products that will interest as many customers as possible. For the most part, manufacturers have this business focus although the driver of their success isn't always the product they produce. Take Harley-Davidson. Yes, they might produce motorcycles but they sell what has been described as the Harley mystique – apparel, road rallies, accessories, and a rebel lifestyle even for the 57-year-old man in a small midwestern town.

◆ **Customer focus.** We're talking here about learning as much about a customer as possible, then finding a way to satisfy their needs and expectations through a variety of products and services. A case in point is Nike. Nike makes sports shoes but it also makes outerwear, luggage, game equipment, and lots more for high-performance athletes.

◆ **Technology focus.** Maybe a better term might be innovation because products in this category might either sell technology or use it in innovative ways. We tend to think of the Dells and the IBMs and the Sonys but 3M also fits this category, using its coating and bonding processes to create myriad products, from adhesive tapes to Post-It notes, to fabric protectors, to surgeon's tape, to (would you believe?) furnace filters.

◆ **Distribution focus.** Mary Kay would be a case in point. It has a very unique sales approach. Its channel of distribution is the secret to its success – and the many fat bank accounts of housewives and others who sell cosmetics as Mary Kay representatives. The company may produce the products it sells or not but critical to its growth is its ability to market its products in a hearty single channel or multiple ones.

When you consider this list of growth drivers or strategic purposes in terms of Amazon.com, not only is it evident that Amazon.com's growth driver or strategic purpose is to address the needs of customers, but also that its choice to expand its offerings parallels Nike. Both have targeted a specific customer – in Nike's case, it is male and female athletes; in Amazon's case, it is high-tech types in the middle and upper classes. But both also sell a range of products, and those products widely differ – Nike offers sports shoes and luggage while Amazon markets books and pet food. Yet both have a similar goal – which is to treat the customer extremely well.

> **"Strategic triage demands tough decisions about which opportunities to pursue."**

Decisions that Jeff Bezos makes to grow his business would seem to be prompted by that issue. With multiple opportunities available to him, he appears to choose those that most satisfy his targeted audiences. And keep in mind that his Web site provides him with considerable data about that audience. As individuals order products or otherwise interact with his cyberstore, they provide information about their interests. In that respect, the site acts as a continuous survey instrument.

# FOCUS ON THE INVESTING PHASE

Jeff Bezos clearly still sees Amazon.com in the investing phase. His goal is to grow the Web site, adding various reasons in the form of products and services for visitors to come to his cyberstore. His focus remains the same, and he has kept that focus by:

◆ **Maintaining his vision.** From the time he and his wife Mackenzie and their dog drove west, Jeff Bezos had a clear idea about the kind of business he wanted to create on the Web. Decisions he has made since the launching of the site reflect that vision. He's been careful not to be tempted by the easy picking of low-hanging fruits that might send him off in other directions. He's avoided this by adhering as closely to the original business plan as external circumstances have allowed, building a team on whose judgment he can depend, and weighing each and every decision against its value to long-term growth.

◆ **Focusing on value streams.** Each company has its strengths – value streams or chains that contribute to its competitiveness. Bezos' company has its logistics, which allows it to sell and se-curely deliver product without maintaining major inventory, and customer value proposition built on five traditional values and the added one of "shoptainment."

◆ **Having a clear sense of purpose.** You can have a vision but that vision can become complicated in time with bottom line is-sues. Better to have a sense of purpose around which others can rally, as Bezos has. His clear sense of purpose is to change the way people shop by creating a model on the Web. And his senior staff and employees are committed to that same purpose.

◆ **Defining opportunities.** Data collected from customers enable Amazon.com to identify products to add to their offerings and also identify services they can provide to encourage further traffic on their site. It doesn't hurt, either, that Bezos has assembled a team of individuals who are familiar with the needs of prospective customers because they are representative of those customers. Bezos works hard not to allow the competition to drive him to short-term actions that could impede long-term goals.

◆ **Practising triage.** There are numerous opportunities. But a lean business on the Web knows that it can go in only so many directions. Further, triage demands guidelines. In medicine, it's a matter of survival. In business, triage is based on corporate focus, whether product, customer, technology, or distribution channel. For Bezos, the key is customer satisfaction and strategic plans are made, and tactics are set, based on that.

◆ **Focusing on the value proposition.** Different organizations operate on various value propositions *vis à vis* customers. At Amazon.com, traditional values are important – like issues of cost, quality, speed of delivery, service, and innovation – but e-commerce isn't traditional business. The value proposition is "shoptainment" for Amazon.com, services and products offered to bring people to the Web site for the purpose of encouraging them to buy. Think P.T. Barnum's sideshows to get people to buy a ticket to get into the main tent. Barnum knew how to draw people in his day, and Jeff Bezos knows how to draw them in the new millennium.

# FOCUS ON THE VALUE PROPOSITION

Throughout this book we have talked about the customer value proposition. Aptly enough in a chapter entitled "Focus," we need to focus further on that to understand some of the decisions Bezos has made. Customer value is defined by several factors, including cost, quality, speed of delivery, service during the interaction with the company, and innovation. Just as we looked at growth drivers to give us insights into decisions made by Amazon.com, let's look at these traditional value propositions:

◆ **Costs.** Customers want to pay the least money for some product or service yet get the same quality. Human nature is such that people won't expect quality to exceed standard if the item is priced lower. And promises of such aren't believed.

◆ **Quality.** Where quality is most important, often price is not. People expect to pay to get the "very best" of something. In fact, where quality is an issue, people question whether they are getting the quality promised in marketing ads if price is not at a level to justify the quality promised.

◆ **Speed.** Companies that can provide quick delivery are practicing this value proposition. People don't like to wait for something they have ordered. If ordering in a catalog would mean a month-long wait, many would choose to buy the item in a retail store or another catalog firm that promises quick turnaround. The issue of speed has prompted many catalog distributors to provide Federal Express at no additional charge.

◆ **Service repair and replacement.** People want to feel that they can call a company at any time – 24 hours a day even – to address a problem and get someone on the phone whose manner suggests she or he is willing to help.

◆ **Innovation.** In the computer field, people want the fastest, the newest, the most advanced technology. Which is why Dell continually reinvents its products, introducing new features to attract and keep customers. But innovation-anchored companies aren't only high-tech firms. Earlier, I mentioned 3M. This company truly falls into this category, as does Rubbermaid. And so does Amazon.com.

Actually, Amazon.com practises all five traditional value propositions. It offers discounting on its books and recently was accused in the press of beginning a price war with brick-and-mortar bookstores to provide best-sellers at reduced costs. Quality of service is something that Amazon.com offers with its 1-Click™ proprietary software. Likewise, its personalization of service once a visitor has purchased from the site. Large-scale distribution centers throughout the US and the world are designed to ensure speedier and more secure delivery of products purchased from Amazon.com. Amazon.com is available 24 hours a day and, despite heavy traffic, downloads quickly and services visitors ably. Innovative technology, built or purchased through acquisitions, not only ensures that it is ahead of the technology curve but also communicates that fact to surfers who tend to be interested in that issue – and likely to visit as a consequence.

But Amazon.com practises a Web-based value proposition for visitors – something Bezos once called "shoptainment." In short, the value proposition it would seem to be promoting is that customers should have fun when they shop. Which explains the multiple reviews, eBay-type auctions, and greeting cards you can send to friends with or without Amazon.com products.

Early retailers learned the value of storefront windows to draw customers in. Many of Bezos' decisions have made his Web page into the equivalent of a storefront window with lots of merchandise to draw the viewer in. Links to other merchandise for sale adds to the convenience of shopping at the site. It's like visiting a mall on the Web, with links to various shops from your favorite entertainment store (where you buy books, videos, and CDs). Which is what Amazon.com purports to be.

**Bezos says the business plan calls for investment heavily in the long term – "ten-plus" years.**

As we hear about one purchase by Amazon.com and then another, it's easy to be fooled into believing that the organization is not pursuing a steady course. But that is exactly what the organization is doing. It would seem to be ultimately aiming at becoming a destination site for various businesses – including itself. And it is very likely to be just that because Bezos has planned for it.

## BIBLIOGRAPHY

Anonymous (1998) "Does Amazon.com really matter?" *Forbes*, April 6.

Wood, James B. and Rothstein, Larry (1999) *The Next Level: Essential Strategies for Achieving Breakthrough Growth*. Perseus Books.

de Jonge, Peter. (1999) "Riding the wild, perilous waters of Amazon.com," *New York Times Magazine*, March 14.

Four

# BRAND THE SITE

"Marketing and innovation produce results, all the rest are 'costs.' "
**Peter F. Drucker, *People and Performance***

Branding is important to soups, salad dressings, and other items in a grocery store, washing machines and dish washers in an appliance store, and even used sedans, station wagons, and suburban vans in a dealer's lot. It creates in customers' minds the idea that there is no product quite like it. A brand is an efficient way to sell; a strong brand name doesn't make marketing superfluous but it can make it easier. A weak or poor brand name may make all the advertising, sales promotion, and public relations you do worthless.

Most of us know the worth of branding to traditional retail, but few see its value to e-commerce. Jeff Bezos has recognized it all along, and he has used branding to make Amazon.com into one of the hottest retail sites in cyberspace. As evidence of the power of brand-centered buying on the Web, consider that consumers today purchase cars from Web sites without ever seeing the cars, going for a test drive, or kicking the tires. On the Web, products can be branded or, as in the case of Amazon.com, sites can be branded.

## PROMOTING CYBERBUZZ

Bezos considers branding even more important in e-retail than in traditional retail. One reason may be the impact of "cyberbuzz" – those continuous communications among Internet users in newsgroups or online forums about their site experiences. Word of mouth is much more powerful online than offline. A customer of a traditional retailer might tell five people about

# BEZOS' BRANDING
# SECRETS

What does Bezos know about branding on the Web that others might not? The Bezos school of branding advises:

◆ **Grow brand name today** to move more merchandise tomorrow. That would seem to be Jeff Bezos's thinking. Although he has grown his store to include more than books, he has not differentiated his book division from his music line or from his video line. And he has not done so deliberately. Think about Chevrolet or American Express, or Levi Strauss, or Procter & Gamble. Each has grown by extending its line of products or services, each with its own brand name: Chevy has ten car models; American Express offers an assortment of cards and services; Levi Strauss offers jeans of different styles and cuts; and Procter & Gamble has varied toothpastes. Each model or product name has undermined the power of the brand. For instance, Levi Strauss can now fit any and all; in being able to do this, however, it would seem to have lost half of its market share.

◆ **Understand what is behind your brand identity.** Some marketers might argue that Bezos is making a mistake by expanding the line of products he is selling and thereby diluting the value of his organization's association with books. In the beginning, that might have been true – that is, when Amazon.com was first launched as an online bookstore. But as the site has grown, it has come to be associated more with values like its wide array of product for sale and its discounted prices, and its safe and secure delivery of sales items. In this respect, Amazon is comparable to Starbucks, which offers 30 coffees without diluting its brand name because its name is its brand and its brand is built around its ambiance.

◆ **Make public relations as important as advertising.** If advertising doesn't grow market share, at least it helps sustain it. Public relations can build a new brand and maintain that growth by continuing to familiarize potential customers with the product. In the case of Amazon, public relations (think "cyberbuzz") played a tremendous role in its early success and continues to do so, as visitors to the Web read messages from Jeff Bezos about new members of Amazon's Associates Program.

◆ **Make your name mean something.** Think about Q-Tips or Kleenex, or Xerox, or Scotch tape. These names have come to stand for an entire line of products, first and foremost, because they were the first ones in the marketplace. But beyond that, the name or marketing effort behind it linked the product to its purpose. Which is the secret of Amazon. Just as promotional copy for Kleenex, when first sold, advised, "Don't put a cold in your pocket," Amazon.com promised to be "the largest bookstore in the world." That promise can be extended to "the world's largest selection."

◆ **Share the wealth.** Hotlinks on a Web may be equivalent to multiple stores in a mall. Amazon.com could have added off-the-shelf drug store items to its product line and sold them itself but rather it has chosen to make a visit to Amazon.com more purposeful by linking to DrugStore.com. It knew that it would not have the credibility that the other e-tailer has to extend its product line to drugs, but a hotlink to DrugStore.com on its site adds reason to visit Amazon.com. A comparable example is how Starbucks fits so comfortably in Barnes & Noble bookstores, providing a unique value to the chain.

◆ **Recognize that service quality is a perception,** not necessarily a reality. While Amazon.com does indeed deliver on its promises of a huge inventory of products, secure payment procedures, and speedy delivery, quality, as a value, is something that is truly measurable only in the minds of visitors to the site. To sustain the positive image, Amazon.com has continued to upgrade

> the site, adding not only new products available at the site but also content beyond products on sale to give potential customers reason to come to the site.
>
> ◆ **Deliver what the brand name promises.** It's easy to forget the basics as you expand the business. If you plan to do business on the Web, it's critical to remember the power of cyberbuzz. Word of mouth multiplies many, many times that offline. Don't lose a good brand name by bad customer service.

her experience but someone on the "net might tell 5000 or more people through Usenet news groups and listservers about a poor shopping experience. "Cyberbuzz" may have enabled Amazon to hurdle obstacles like no pre-existing distribution relationships and customer insecurities about making purchases online. The site's huge catalog of books, the ease with which it can be searched, and that a discounted book can be delivered in three days has made online customers coo about the site. Surfers who stumbled on it, bookmarked it. When Yahoo! put Amazon.com on its "What's Cool" page for almost a year, that didn't hurt either.

# DON'T FORGET TRADITIONAL MARKETING

Because of initial marketing efforts supplemented with cyberbuzz during its first year in business, Amazon.com was able to turn over inventory 42 times in 1997 compared with Barnes and Noble's 2.1 times. By spring 1998, Amazon.com had 1.5 million customers. In less than two years, Amazon's reputation as e-retailer (or e-tailer to other online retailers) opened the virtual store's door to opportunities beyond books to CDs, then videos, then computer software and hardware. In early 1999, pharmaceuticals were added to the product mix. Before that were pet supplies. Now you can buy groceries on a visit to Amazon.

## KEEP YOUR SLICE OF A BIGGER PIE

While speculations begun after its first year in business continue – earlier thoughts included the idea that ultimately Amazon would get into the publishing business with digitally distributed books and even that some time in the future Amazon.com would build or buy a chain of stores to go along with its online business – they have changed, and now industry watchers see it becoming an online Wal-Mart, offering a wide array of discounted products, or alternatively predicting that Amazon's goal is to become a portal. That Amazon.com is not out to become solely the biggest bookstore or music store is a foregone conclusion. That it has plans to continue to grow would also seem a foregone conclusion. Questioned right after he added CDs to his site, Bezos pointed out that e-commerce was "a big arena. It isn't a winner-take-all kind of business. These are very large markets, and there is room for multiple winners." The more products you can sell without the cost of bricks and mortar – the economic premise behind Amazon – the more profitable it will eventually become. But in the interim, as much money as can be allocated to it is being spent on branding and marketing and advertising. The issue of corporate profitability may hang over Amazon.com, but Bezos has told the business press that he is more concerned about branding his Web site. This continues to be his goal, even as the business enters its fourth year.

# PROMOTE BRANDING AS A CORPORATE VALUE

For 1999, Amazon has alerted investors that it expects marketing and sales expenses to increase significantly. Money managers predict a 50 percent increase, to $200 million. Bezos wants to increase market share while the cost of acquiring it is relatively cheap. While this may mean operating a lean business, even offering below-market salaries supplemented with equity in the business, Bezos has his eye on the longer-term gains. Unlike Bill Gates, he didn't have to be persuaded about the worth of an integrated marketing effort.

> Bezos told *Brandweek*, "Brands to a certain degree are like quick-drying cement. When they're young, they're stretchable and pliant, but over time they become more and more associated with a particular thing and harder to stretch."

The story goes that would-be multi-billionaire Bill Gates questioned the value of advertising and that Jerry Gibbons, then president of Doyle Dane Bernbach, demonstrated its worth by drawing a pie diagram on a cocktail napkin and a piece out of the pie to show Gates his company's current share. Then Gibbons drew a larger circle to illustrate the difference between $1.5 billion and $5 billion and he told Gates that the industry would be growing in the years to come and how now was the time to capture as much share as he could. The cost of acquisition would grow as the market grew. If Gates could increase share now, his firm would be competitive now and in the future. All he would need to do would be to "protect your share."

Gates subsequently doubled his advertising budget.

Based on branding, Amazon's integrating marketing communications effort enables the organization to extend the reach of a traditional advertising effort, simultaneously accomplishing both short- and long-term business needs. Bezos's brand and marketing communications effort is built around four elements: a name that conveys his strategic purpose, short-term and long-term; a satisfying, convenient shopping experience that cultivates customer loyalty; self-effacing ads in carefully targeted media; and hotlinks on commercial sites of all sizes to attract Web shoppers.

## NAME THE COMPANY TO FIT THE IMAGE YOU WANT

Corporate lore says Bezos initially planned to name the Web site "Cadabra," as in "Abracadabra," but Bezos, an Internet brandmeister, would have seemed more likely to have called the site "Abra …" etc., to benefit from the alphabetized lists used to navigate the Web. Prior to the launch, reportedly three months were spent searching for the right name, and that search focused on words that began with "A" so that the site would appear at the top of search engine lists. The goal was to find an "A …" name that was short and memorable, that captured the spirit of the site, and most important that conveyed great size. Hence, Amazon.com. Just as Steve Jobs is said to have named his company after a visit to the All-One Farm in Oregon – because, to him, the apple is the perfect fruit and he wanted Apple to be the perfect company – so Bezos wanted his company to be "Earth's Biggest Bookstore," carrying much more than any conventional bookstore. As Amazon's product

# THERE'S MORE TO A BRAND THAN A NAME

Philip Kotler, in his book *Kotler on Marketing: How to Create, Win and Dominate Markets,* points out that, despite all the to-do about naming a product or service or company, brand experience has to match the brand image for branding to work. "Much," he writes, "can go wrong." Kotler uses the example of a fine brand of canned soup described in a full-color ad in a glitzy magazine, yet is found in a dented and dusty condition on the bottom shelf of your local grocery. Likewise a disgruntled registration clerk can sour the impression you got when you saw a picture of the ritzy hotel in an issue of a classy magazine. And efforts to suggest product quality by a small appliance dealer, says Kotler, count for nought if the appliance you ordered is received damaged – even if the damage was due to shoddy parcel services, not careless packaging by the shipping clerk.

Kotler's conclusion: "Brand building calls for more than brand image building. It calls for managing every *brand contact* that the customer might have with the brand." Which may explain Jeff Bezos' dual focus at Amazon.com: branding and customer satisfaction.

line has grown, the name is still meaningful. Today, Amazon.com no longer stands for "The World's Largest Bookstore" but for "The World's Largest Selection."

The rule for naming a product or store, or Web site, would seem simple: choose a name that captures the product's essence or inspires the imagination, or uniqueness. Some clear-cut names of stores include FindersKeepers, a Florida-based collectibles store; Furniture Medic, a Rhode Island-based furniture restoration firm; and Ebbets Field Flannels, a Washington State-based distributor of historic baseball apparel. Polaroid's Captiva conveys the instant camera's unique ability to "hold captive" life's experiences and provide "captivating images." Compare that to the Mercury Mountaineer, whose name clearly defines it as an off-road transport vehicle but fails to differentiate it from other such cars, like Honda Passport and Subaru Forester. Ocuhist is a product to ease eye discomfort from allergies but the word, while a logical combination of two words associated with its purpose (oculist and histamine), fails to flow on the tongue, while Visine (think vision), also produced by Pfizer, not only conveys its use in helping people with eye irritations but, phonetically speaking, works.

# UNDERSTAND WHAT'S IN A BRAND NAME

What about Web site names? The same rules apply. Names have to sound fresh and new even if the site duplicates one already on the Web. Names should stir the imagination or otherwise gain a surfer's attention. Further, site names should be as simple as possible, they should be believable, and they should be easy to pronounce, pleasing to the ear, easy to spell and therefore easy to look up on a search engine. For instance, you might think spelling critters with a *k* makes your online petcare product firm kritterkare creative, but you'd likely lose or irritate customers who couldn't find it in search engines or phone directories if you also run a retail outlet.

What about acronyms? If the name can't be pronounced as an acronym, the initials should make sense to someone navigating the Web. Take the Web site www.igogolf. When David

Schofman came up with the name, he was relating it to the name of his company International Golf Outlet, not considering whether it would be easy for prospective customers to find it on the Web. So it came as a surprise, he said, when a Japanese customer e-mailed him congratulations on the creativity of his site name. On the other hand, as his business is getting off the ground, he is sorry he hadn't named the site the readily found URL golf.com. Reel.com's founder, Stuart Skorman, came up with a site name which makes clear his site's product line (videos) but it doesn't make clear the size of its inventory – 85,000 videos of which a little less than half can be rented by mail, cross referenced by 32 categories, which makes it the biggest video store on the Web. Another site, www.hothothot.com, which sells hot, spicy sauces, has received e-mail messages from disgruntled visitors who expected a different site experience. Likewise, www.gamesville.com, which would suggest a retailer of "Shoots and Ladders," "Candyland," "Trouble," and other board games at discounted prices but which is actually the site of an advertisement-supported Web game show where visitors can play games like *Jeopardy* and *Wheel of Fortune* and win cash prizes.

## LEND CREDENCE TO THE BRAND NAME

So site names are important but what the names stand for may be even more important, above and beyond the products they offer. Bezos has compared branding to quick-drying cement, noting that when firms are young they can be pliant, but over time "they become more and more associated with a particular thing and harder to stretch." That his site is known for its rich selection of products and high level of service, he said, would allow its extension of product lines. This aspect of Amazon's customer-centric culture will be addressed in the next chapter, but quality of service prominently figures in perception of a brand. Starbucks founder Howard Schultz has said about the impact of service on brand, "Starbucks success proves that a multimillion-dollar advertising program isn't a prerequisite for building a national brand – nor are the deep pockets of a big corporation. You can do it one customer at a time, one store at a time, one market at a time." Amazon.com has connected with customers beyond its catalog of books that would, in print, equal seven telephone directories or its humungous inventory of CDs or videos, or other products. America Online calls its computer bulletin board a community, and visitors to Amazon.com, likewise, have this same sense of community. Bezos has said that Amazon's customers want selection, good service, and low prices. If it is to compete with big world brands, it has to be better in each of these three areas. But Amazon's "value-added proposition" is more. Yes, it is quality service, but this customer satisfaction may be short-lived. On the other hand, the sense of community that occurs from a consistently pleasant shopping experience lasts a long, long time, brings you back time and time again, and encourages you to share your experience with others. Chuck Pettis, a principal with Floathe Johnson, an advertising and public relations agency, suggests client firms model the mental and emotional process customers follow when making product

> Amazon.com entices prospective members to its Associates Program by telling them, "Our experience in building online stores will help you build a first-class store on your site." In other words, join the affiliate program and grow big fast, like Amazon.

purchases. The ladder contains rungs labeled "emotional value," "job value," "benefit," and "feature or attribute." If you used this process with Amazon.com, the feature might be "huge selection;" the benefit would be "reliability" (the site has only been down twice in its history to date); and job value might be "fast delivery" or "accessibility of hard-to-find books," or "ease in identifying unknown titles," but the emotional value might be "fun" from reading reviews and authors' interviews, or posting one's own opinion.

## DON'T FORGET TRADITIONAL ADVERTISING

The majority of customers are believed to come to the site through word of mouth. But this has not precluded the use of advertisements on television or in print. Barnes and Noble's decision to sell books online as well as in outlets led to a series of irreverent brand-oriented radio and television ads that showed the Statue of Liberty and Seattle's Space Needle drowning in books. Print ads have appeared in *People* and *Entertainment Weekly,* such placements clear indication that Amazon.com clients, while book buyers, are more likely to be reading these periodicals than the Sunday book supplements of major newspapers. Amazon.com buyers are slightly more affluent and technologically inclined than average buyers.

## ADVERTISE ON THE WEB, OF COURSE

Besides print ads, there are advertising banners in high-traffic Web sites. Amazon also has them on Yahoo! and AOL, swapped in return for literary content. And then there are the "Letters from Jeff Bezos," thousands and thousands of messages that reinforce the quality of service available from Amazon.com in the course of alerting you to the fact that another Web site has joined Amazon.com's "Associates Program," a network of more than 60,000 Web sites from which you can order books from Amazon and more than 100,000 Web sites from which you can order CDs from Amazon.

## CROSS-BRAND

Information on the affiliate program is on Amazon.com's Web site. Commercial sites that sign up can earn 15 percent of sales on the more than 400,000 book titles and 5 percent or more on the 1.1 million additional in-print titles, CDs, videos, and other products. Not only is participation in the program financially rewarding to affiliates but member sites are able to bond with their own customers at no extra costs through the program.

Members of the affiliate program include sites of all sizes – not just smaller commercial sites. Among the big music sites are Spin, Vibes, and Spinner.com. Reba McEntire's Web site, TheDoors.com, and Mojo Records are also sites. There are also fan sites, concert promoters, orchestras and event halls, radio stations, and broadcast talk-show sites in the music

> Bezos told *Forbes*, "We had a world-class site the day we launched – but it was only a tenth as good as the site we have now. And we relied on word of mouth to build brand awareness, so we didn't have to do much advertising. That's not possible anymore."

associates program. Within the book program are even search engines like Yahoo!, AOL.com, Netscape, Excite!, and Alta Vista. First of the big portals to sign was Yahoo! in July 1997. Then, Yahoo! was the world's single largest Internet navigational guide, with the broadest, most comprehensive, and easiest access to information on the Web. The agreement gave Amazon.com direct links from every Yahoo! search result and book category page. Besides a hotlink on each page of Yahoo!, the deal with the search engine, of course, meant extensive promotional exposure throughout Yahoo!

What made Yahoo! agree to the deal? The same reason that other sites have joined with Amazon. Bezos' site is a recognized leader on the Internet. No matter your own positioning, being associated with a "leader," with a reputation for quality and innovation, is valuable – heck, it's priceless.

## THE BATTLE OF THE BOOKSTORES

Although Amazon.com is clearly no longer only a bookstore, the competitors most mentioned by Amazon.com watchers are still the online sites for Barnes and Noble and Borders. How do they stand up to Amazon.com?

BarnesandNoble.com and Bol.com offer the same capability as Amazon.com in allowing visitors to search for a specific title or collection of book titles, either by title, author, or ISBN; like Amazon.com, they sell their products at discounted prices, and they promise excerpts from new books, interviews, and other "shopertainment" (a Bezos term) as you browse the site. They even have the ability to personalize orders once you make a purchase.

Like Amazon.com, which has broadened its product offerings to include CDs and videos, among other products, Borders also markets CDs and videos from its site; BarnesandNoble.com doesn't offer videos or CDs, although some of its real-time stores sell CDs, but it offers hotlinks to magazine titles for sale and sells computer software from its site. Amazon.com has a link to enable it to sell computer software from its site but it doesn't market magazines – at least not yet.

I like the speed of Amazon.com and dislike the me-too look of BarnesandNoble.com. As one reporter noted, "feature for feature, service for service, discount for discount, even annoyance for annoyance, BarnesandNoble.com has become a close match for Internet pioneer Amazon.com." Bol.com doesn't look like either of the other two but it is learning from both; many of the programs it offers to other Web sites (like its Associates Program and LinkShare) resemble programs initially offered at Amazon.com and now offered by both Amazon and B&N. Which site would I most use to purchase books? None. I live only two blocks away from one major Barnes and Noble outlet and only ten blocks from another Barnes and Noble store, and have several category book stores nearby, too. I live in a big city with many alternatives to the Web, which makes me a tough candidate to buy books other than hard-to-find topics from any Web bookstore. On the other hand, I have to credit Barnes & Noble for how quickly it is catching up with Amazon.com, thereby demonstrating how competitive advantages based on technology can so quickly disappear.

Because of my nearness to two Barnes and Noble stores, when I do have to order online, I admit to a preference for BarnesandNoble.com, since they can get books to me faster than Amazon. On the other hand, I enjoy the editorial content of Amazon.com, and I will research titles and order hard-to-find books from it.

Of the three sites, graphically I prefer the look of Bol.com. Perhaps because it is younger than the other two sites, it has yet to add all the bells and whistles that make for a cluttered look. I found it hard to get to the home page of BarnesandNoble.com, whereas I found both Bol.com's and Amazon.com's home pages easily accessed. On its home page, Bol.com refers to itself as a "community," which is a term that many sites seem to use, including BarnesandNoble.com and Amazon.com, but Bol.com mentions an Info Desk staff (does this mean "real-time people?") who will try to help if you can't recall the title of the book or the author but know that there was a man and a collie and some scenery that could be Scotland in the background (*Lassie*, maybe?).

Still, the battle would seem to be between BarnesandNoble.com and Amazon.com. Barnes and Noble planned to purchase America's largest wholesaler, Ingram Book Group, which fills more than 50 percent of Amazon.com orders. While Barnes and Noble said that its acquisition would not change the availability of books to Amazon.com, Bezos quickly indicated plans to diversify sources, for clearly, acquisition by Barnes and Noble of its chief supplier of books could change the economic model by which Amazon.com operates. In June 1999, Barnes and Noble called off the $600 million acquisition following rumors that the government competition regulator, the Federal Trust Commission, planned to oppose the deal. Aside from this issue, however, there are four other factors that will influence who wins the "battle of the bookstores:"

The credence Barnes and Noble puts on projections about the growth of e-commerce versus traditional retail. If they agree that e-commerce will replace most retail operations except last-minute convenience shopping, they will need to reconsider the role of BarnesandNoble.com. In an interview, Jeff Killeen, president and CEO of BarnesandNoble.com described the site as an extension of the larger store, "another channel of distribution."

BarnesandNoble.com recognize that e-commerce is very different from traditional retail. Asked what he felt was the biggest obstacle to growth online, Killeen spoke about the need for "online book lovers to know that they can always come to BarnesandNoble.com for an unparalleled user experience, for superior online selection, and service as well as unequaled price and value." He points to Barnes and Noble's brand as a real-time bookstore, whereas Bezos reminds us that his firm has been on the Web for several years. "We will continue to focus on providing the technology and service that give our customers the very best *online* shopping experience," said Bezos. "We're not a stationary target," he continued. "We were blessed with a two-year head start, and our goal is to increase that gap."

BarnesandNoble.com's reality is as one division of a giant chain. Amazon.com not only has a clarity of purpose – e-commerce – and the money to invest in brand enhancement – it also does not have to go through the chain of command of a much larger organization to get approval to make course corrections, as BarnesandNoble.com likely has to do even though its business is so different from that of the parent. Bezos commented: "We're going to be focused exclusively on selling books online, whereas Borders, and Barnes and Noble are going to have to worry about two things: They're going to have to figure out how to sell books in the physical world, which is a hard thing to do by itself, and they're going to have to figure out how to do a great job of selling books online."

Bezos' future plans. As we get a better idea of where Bezos ultimately wants to take Amazon.com, we may discover that Bezos's competitors are not BarnesandNoble.com or Bol.com but, instead, the new online Wal-Mart or Yahoo!, AOL, and other Web portals.

# BIBLIOGRAPHY

Jeffrey, Don (1998) "Amazon.com eyes retailing music online: major player's entry will raise competitive stakes," *Billboard*, January 31.

Anonymous (1998) "Does Amazon.com really matter? *Forbes*, April 6.

Anonymous (1998) "Jeff Bezos: discounter," *Brandweek*, October 12.

Anonymous (1997) "Jeffrey Bezos," Chain Store Age Executive with Shopping Center Age, December.

Kotler, Philip (1999) *Kotler on Marketing: How to Create, Win and Dominate Markets*, Free Press, New York.

Delano, Frank (1999) *The Omnipowerful Brand*, Amacom, New York.

Gimein, Mark (1999) "Playing the Net Stock Game" *The Industry Standard: The Newsmagazine of the Internet Economy*, January 18. http:///www.thestandard.net/articles

Easton, Jacklyn (1999) *StrikingItRich.Com*, McGraw-Hill, New York.

Pettis, Chuck (1995) *Technobrands: How to Create & Use "Brand Identity" to Market, Advertise & Sell Technology Products*, Amacom, New York.

Five

# GET AND KEEP CUSTOMERS BY OFFERING GREAT VALUE

"Treat the customer as an appreciating asset."
**– Tom Peters, *Thriving on Chaos***

Cyberbuzz attracts prospective buyers to Amazon. But customer loyalty has built it into the popular online superstore it is. Of the company's eight million customers, from more than 160 countries, more than half are repeat buyers. And with cause. Bezos has built Amazon.com into a customer-centric organization, which means that the goal of everyone in the organization is to ensure that its customers are satisfied.

# PRACTISE CUSTOMER-CENTRICITY

For a retail organization that is watching every dollar to enhance brand and maximize marketing, with stiff competition already present and more on the horizon, customer-centricity is essential. In the sense that customer service is solely the processing of orders, it doesn't mean exceptional service; customer satisfaction is the product of service at or beyond customer expectations. And exceptional service helps you to retain customers and even develop relationships with them so that they aren't lured away by competitors offering lower prices. Dollarwise, replacing customers lost to competitors is five to six times more costly, maybe more, than retaining existing customers. While Amazon.com is presently in a sowing, not harvesting, phase, and would seem focused on extending product offerings to increase traffic to its site, keeping current customers satisfied would logically be the second part of a two-prong strategy. Customer retention is a driver of net growth.

One consulting firm projects that retention of 5 percent of a company's customer base can increase profitability by as much as 125 percent.

Honda provides an excellent example of the strategic benefits of customer retention. Although the organization spends far less on advertising than do other Japanese car makers in the US, it is also the largest foreign supplier of cars in the US, in major part because it is ranked number one in repurchase loyalty, with a 68 percent repurchase rate for existing customers. A comparison of advertising expenditures by Honda, Toyota, Nissan also brings home the dollar savings in advertising from customer retention, with Honda spending only $150 per car on advertising and its Japanese competitors Toyota and Nissan at $300 and $400 respectively.

## KNOW THY CUSTOMERS

Amazon processes orders and ships books, CDs, and videos, and it does these things well. But satisfaction comes from understanding customer expectations and meeting or exceeding these. Bezos expects this level of service from his employees, for his online store demands it. Through customer satisfaction, the e-retailer can move first-time buyers up to loyal customers, to allies, and eventually to evangelists. And as Bezos has said, "a pool of evangelists will use the Internet as a megaphone to help attract new customers with word of mouth."

Bezos told *Forbes*, "There are three things our customers want: selection, ease of use, and low prices."

# SING THE PRAISES OF YOUR CUSTOMERS

Amazon.com sings its own praises, too, posting positive feedback from customers on its site. Customers praise the firm's site for speedy delivery of their order, the ability to get them books inaccessible elsewhere – even from the publisher – the e-mail follow up that alerts customers to the status of their orders, priority mail delivery, and well-designed, easy-to-use purchasing procedures. Each of these elements could be seen as components of a value chain or stream, designed for the sole purpose of delighting customers. Creating such a chain is easier than reinventing existing procedures, which may give Amazon.com a competitive advantage over new-to-the-Web competitors that must rethink traditional customer service to equal Amazon.com's handling of orders. Even so, Amazon.com, once having set expectations, must continue to meet them. Which can be difficult on occasion.

# GO TO EXTRAORDINARY MEASURES TO KEEP YOUR PROMISES

During the 1998 holiday season, employees from all departments and all levels – including, yes, senior management – helped out in the firm's Seattle distribution center to ensure products got to their purchasers in time for gift giving. Part of the company's "customers first" thinking, salaried employees got time off from their regular jobs to work the stacks. Hourly employees were paid overtime. Modeling the behavior so important to the company's customer service image were Bezos and other company officers who were also in the distribution center, or manning customer calls. A swing-shift manager at the firm's Seattle distribution center observed, "It didn't matter the time of day or the difficulty of the task ... there were always workers from other departments who helped. We counted on their help, and they made a tangible difference for our customers."

It was a busy season. More than one million new customers purchased from Amazon. In one day, the firm shipped more than $6 million in products. Over the season, sales were four times that of the previous year.

Such volume coincided with the addition of a third distribution facility, this time in Nevada, to speed deliveries to customers on the west coast. Amazon already has state-of-the-art centers in Washington State and Delaware. (We will look at the place of this distribution network beyond its contribution to customer satisfaction in Chapter 8.)

# BEZOS' CUSTOMER-VALUE PROPOSITION

If Jeff Bezos was to conduct a course on customer satisfaction for Web stores, here are some elements he'd include in his curriculum:

◆ **Leave visitors to the site with a positive impression.** Even if they don't buy on their first visit there, surfers are likely to bookmark the site for that time when they need a book in a hurry. The entertaining content draws them to the site and the services offered bring them back when they are looking for a hard-to-find book or album, when they need to know what books are available on a specific subject before making a purchasing decision, or they live too far from a bookstore to make a trip convenient.

◆ **Give potential buyers other reasons for visiting the store.** This is important to Web retailers. Besides selling the product itself, they have to sell the sizzle of doing business on the Web. Amazon.com entices visitors by reviews, contests, and other events and offerings beyond the products it sells. Likewise Software.net, an Internet-based computer software store where users can browse, purchase, and retrieve software electronically. At Software.net, users can access a variety of software-related information, including product reviews and marketing materials. Over 6500 software titles are available for purchase, either through an 800 number or credit card number online. Like Amazon.com, Software.net also acts as distributor, without inventory of all the software it supplies in stock at all times. In that respect, it is less a store and more information resource about software. Which makes for repeat visitors. An independent camera and photo store in Fremont, Ohio, Dumminger Photography, overcomes stiff price competition from retail giants by initiating a "shutter bug" club for frequent buyers, processing a free roll of film for every seven taken and donating a camera, film, and processing to every mother who delivers a baby over Mother's Day weekend. At Christmas customers who process a roll of film at his shop are offered a free 5 by 7 picture with Santa, which often prompts them to order photo greeting cards. In these ways, owner Ken Dumminger believes that he sells the "sizzle" of photography.

◆ **Make a customer's encounters with the company a delight.** That delight comes both from the processing of orders and from visits to the site where there are interesting things to read and to do. Great service makes the visit memorable. So does the opportunity to interact with others in forums or by posting personal reviews.

- ◆ **Personalize and customize service.** Visitors to Amazon.com can sign up for personal notification services to stay up-to-date on books for their favorite authors, or receive reviews of exceptional books and albums in categories that interest them. Ebaugh's Gifts, in McPherson, Kansas, sells gifts and collectibles, and it tracks items in each regular customer's collection so there are no duplications, and alerts bosses to upcoming Secretary's Day and asks them if they want to send gift baskets again this year.

- ◆ **Perform as promised.** Most customers complain when the organization from which they bought something overpromised and underdelivered. Amazon.com has set high expectations in its customers but it also has delivered on these.

- ◆ *Exceed expectations.* At Amazon.com, a case in point is the e-mail messages to purchasers that their orders are on their way. Forty percent of www.igo-golf use their online order tracking system. Tracking numbers are given to customers on request and they can monitor their order through the site by clicking on the button for the express delivery service, which displays the order's status but without a tracking number. The Web-based print shop, www.iPrint.com, also gets e-mail queries from customers about the status of orders, but it handles them by providing customers with a reference ID and password that allows them even to cancel an order if it has not yet been sent to the printer.

- ◆ **Communicate the importance of customer satisfaction,** beyond all other values. Bezos does this by word and by deed. Time spent last holiday helping to get product to customers in time for the holidays may say more to associates at Amazon.com than the trimester meetings at which he points to the need to create value for the customer as part of the organization's brand. His strategic commitment is communicated to his management team, employees *and* customers.

◆ **Create ownership.** Employee commitment is tied to customer value, and employee commitment can be built on motivation and ownership. Both of these were discussed in Chapter 2, but it is worth emphasizing that a sense of community among employees can create employee loyalty which can spill over to customer loyalty, as employees pull together to ensure quality of service. Likewise, equity in the business motivates employees to do their utmost to make customers come back.

◆ **Do something better than anyone else does it.** Amazon.com offers "the world's largest selection" at discounted prices with the click of a mouse. For today's overstressed consumers, with little time to shop, access via the Internet to such a wide variety of products without a long delivery wait is a plus. But make the shopping not only easier but pleasurable, and you will get and keep their business. Breed & Co. tries to make a visit to its hardware, lawn, and garden materials store pleasurable by greeting each customer as he or she enters. But that's not all. According to Ann Breed, if a customer needs a new faucet, an employee will show him how to install it. If the customer is elderly, the firm will go out and do it for him.

◆ **Market knowledge as well as product.** Amazon.com provides information for those who can't remember a book or video title or are looking for a sound but don't know exactly what they want. And high school and college students who are doing research for their classroom can identify books for study. Knowledge is also part of the service package that Hahn Appliance Center in Tulsa offers. Which makes it more than competitive with its price-driven larger competitors like Circuit City and Sam's driveo. Unlike comparable sized appliance retailers, they also offer an impressive inventory of refrigerators, stoves, washers, dryers, dishwashers, and microwaves.

# STAY CUSTOMER-OBSESSED; DON'T LET COMPETITORS DISTRACT

Bezos told *Brandweek* a few months earlier: "Businesses can go astray by being competitor-obsessed versus customer-obsessed. You have to find out what customers want and how to give it to them." Another retailer, Sam Walton, agrees. In his book *Made in America,* he wrote: "The secret of successful retailing is to give your customers what they want." At Amazon.com, among other things, customers want delivery as promised. Other Amazon.com customer expectations are convenience (which shopping online from your living room offers), a wide selection of products – Amazon offers 2.5 million titles, including books, CDs, and videos – and a pleasant shopping experience. On the last point, Walton wrote: "You love it when you visit a store that somehow exceeds your expectations, and you hate it when a store inconveniences you, or gives you a hard time, or just pretends you're invisible."

Amazon.com has built customer loyalty by creating a brand that is more than the sum of its parts. Yes, the e-retailer sells books, CDs, videos, and now pharmaceuticals and more, but it also appeals to customers emotionally – on a "feeling good" level. To appreciate the impact of "warm and fuzzy" feelings on consumers, consider the early history of Prodigy and America Online. America Online grew beyond Prodigy – positioned as an information service – when America Online positioned itself as a facilitator of Internet communications, acting as a medium by which people could meet, stay informed, buy products, and learn new things.

Likewise, Amazon.com's positioning. At this online megastore, what does a pleasant shopping experience entail?

## MAKE CUSTOMERS WANT TO RETURN

With two clicks, you tell the search and retrieval system whether you are looking for a book, CD, or video. Then you type in the name of the author or artist or title or, if you aren't sure exactly what you want, the subject matter. The system locates the information you need. You can browse for books in 28 subject areas and music in hundreds of styles. Each book has its own page, and each page contains a picture of the book jacket and price, author's name, publisher, and number of days for delivery. Just below those data is the Amazon.com sales rank for the titles.

This idea of ranking product sales came from Bezos. He had noticed how newspaper and magazine book supplements rank bestselling books weekly. To outdo them, he had a system set up to update Amazon's top 10,000 books hourly. The next 100,000 are updated daily. The remainder are updated every month.

> "The balance of power online shifts away from the merchant to customer – which is a great thing – but the merchant has to recognize it."
> – Bezos

To acknowledge best selling books, the company offers Category Bestseller Awards, recognizing the bestselling publishers and authors in each of 24 book genres, including the arts, music, home and gardening, computers, business and investing, humor, and health. Aside from the pleasure it gives a reader to discover that his or her favorite author is best in a particular category, the program gives authors and publishers "an unrivaled vantage point to gauge how their books are selling, with the appropriate genre, more accurately and more currently than they could find anywhere else."

As you find books, or music CDs, or videos you want to purchase, you click and they are placed in a shopping cart. At the end of your shopping spree, you enter shipping information and your credit card number, or phone or fax number if you prefer. Amazon.com e-mails confirmation when orders are shipped. Products are delivered to one of Amazon.com's distribution centers or warehouses, from where they are shipped. The reassurances Amazon.com offers about using a credit card to put through your order makes e-commerce seem not only easy but safe.

But what customers really like about Amazon.com is the opportunity to check out others' views on books, music, or videos they're considering, as their comments are right there on the screen.

---

## LEARNING FROM THE BEST

In retail, if there is an organization that can set the example for others, it is Wal-Mart. In his book *Made in America,* written shortly before he died, Sam Walton defined ten rules of success. Rule number eight states, "Exceed your customers' expectations. If you do, they'll come back over and over. Give them what they want – and a little more." Based on his leadership of Amazon.com, clearly Bezos would concur with Walton.

When Bezos launched Amazon, he initially had to compete with bookstores that were offering coffee and croissants, later operating hours, and sometimes author readings. Now he has to compete with online stores offering similar discounts as his own online store and real stores with special events and offerings, which has made the issue of customer satisfaction even more important to this young firm. Since the organization went online, it has promised quality service, but the stiff competition has meant translating that phrase into more than its initial offer of discounted prices – as deep as 40 percent – and quality service, even the opportunity to post reviews of items purchased or read others' reviews, or enter forums to chat about a favorite author with other fans.

> "You love it when you visit a store that exceeds your expectations, and you hate it when a store inconveniences you."
> **– Sam Walton**

## INCLUDE INTERACTIVE ELEMENTS ON THE WEB

So far, visitors to Amazon have been given the chance to help finish a chapter of a book by author John Updike, or help Sue Grafton name her next book (N Is for …). If you had a secret desire to write your own comic strip, you could help write the first *Doonesbury* comic strip created online. Ten of the eleven *Doonesbury* panels, drawn exclusively for the online bookstore by Gary Trudeau, were posted and visitors could compete each day to give voice to comic characters by writing the next panel to move the story along. In the Amazon.com Kids section, youngsters were given the opportunity to complete one of two poems from celebrated children's poet Jack Prelutsky in the "Be a Poet" contest. Amazon.com set aside room on its site for Francis Ford Coppola's literary magazine *Zoetrope: All-Story*, where the works of today's best short-story writers are presented. And in Amazon's *"Street Lawyer"* contest a lucky visitor to the site won $25,000 or tuition for one year at a law school, and all John Grisham fans won an advanced peek at the first chapter of his new novel, *The Street Lawyer*.

All of this makes for Amazon's loyal following.

# EIGHT THINGS CUSTOMERS WANT

Studies have been done on how we can get closer to the customer off- and online. From those studies you can identify the following criteria important to consumers. If you have visited Amazon.com, how would you rate it based on these eight elements:

◆ **Availability.** When today's customers want something, they want it now. If it's not immediately available, they will wait but they won't wait long. They are less tolerant of delays; if you have promised to deliver on a specific date, they expect it then. Otherwise, they will go elsewhere for their item.

◆ **Selection.** They not only want to be able to choose either from a catalog or from existing inventory but they want information on their options to help them make the best selection.

◆ **Delivery lead times.** Customers don't only want to get their products quickly but they want their orders well packaged so they arrive safely.

◆ **Quality.** This criterion has changed over the years. No longer are we talking simply about a single product. We are talking about the total buying experience. Which on the Web is based on a variety of factors, from ease of usage of the site, to additional information about the product being ordered, to personalized service.

◆ **Reliability.** Consumers don't want to have a problem with any product or service they purchase. However, if something goes wrong, they want to be assured that the retailer will solve the problem immediately. Their satisfaction isn't based on the resolution of the problem alone; they want to feel that they did not have to *demand* resolution to get it. If they did, they will criticize the service as a whole.

◆ **Service.** Like total quality, service is based on the total buying experience. Today's customers want as much information before making a purchase as you can provide, whether it's a knowledgeable service person or printed information on a Web site about a product for sale. Like quality, service is a factor that can differentiate an organization from its competitors, all other things being equal.

◆ **Customer-friendliness.** In traditional retail, customers don't want to encounter surly sales persons. On the Web, they want to find some fun at the sites from which they make purchases. In both real-time and online retailers, however, customers also want to easily return products without being given a tough time.

◆ **Costs.** While we all tend to be more value conscious than in the past, most customers today will pay more for a product or service if they receive the previously mentioned seven items.

How do you ensure these eight items? Take a tack from Jeff Bezos, who every three months or so holds staff meetings to remind his employees about where attention should rest: on providing value to customers. Delighting customers is a recurring theme in interviews with the press, but it is also a recurring theme in discussions with the workforce.

# BIBLIOGRAPHY

Slovan, Margie (1997) "Bound for the Internet," *Nation's Business*, March.

Anonymous (1998) "Does Amazon.com really matter?" *Forbes*, April 6.

Anonymous (1998) "Jeff Bezos: discounter," *Brandweek*, October 12.

Walton, Sam, with Huey, John (1993) *Made in America*, Bantam Books.

Taylor, Don and Smalling Archer, Jeanne (1994) *Up Against the Wal-Marts: How Your Business Can Prosper in the Shadow of the Retail Giants*, Amacom, New York.

Six

# DEVELOP UNBEATABLE LOGISTICS

"Serve and sell."
**– IBM slogan**

Total Quality Management (TQM) is less written about today – pushed out of management press by newer buzzwords like "team management" and "empowerment," and the newest management fad "knowledge management" – but TQM is a relevant concept in discussion of Amazon.com's distribution network. Success in retail can be defined by seven "R" words:

◆ Right product

   Right location

   Right time

   Right packaging

   Right quantity

   Reasonable price

   Right customer.

The secret of retail is offering the right products in the right location at the right time with the right packaging in the right quantity at a reasonable price to the right customer. Doing this is the ongoing objective of Amazon.com's shipping operation. It is a tough standard for which to aim, but there are catalog retailers that have met the goal, like L. L. Bean, with its 99.9 percent order-fill rate.

Failure to satisfy any one of the seven Rs can lose business. Depending on the nature of the problem, the result can range from an indifferent customer to a hostile one. For instance, you can pass by a clothing store whose merchandise isn't in the latest fashions, but if you order a tool by mail and it comes without key parts, you will call and complain. Likewise if the jams and jellies you order as a gift arrive broken, because the box in which they are packaged isn't sturdy enough to take postal handling, you will call and complain. And don't get me on a soap box about foods that are sold only in family sizes in a huge supermarket only two miles from

**Bezos predicts that "strip malls are history," according to *Wired* senior writer Chip Bayers.**

my vacation home. It makes it necessary for me and my dog to drive four miles out of our way to a small grocery store that caters to weekenders and small families.

## IDENTIFY POINTS OF CONTACT

Jeff Bezos recognizes that his staff have several points-of-contact with customers (or "moments of truth," as SAS might refer to it,) which are critical to quality service. He has worked to ensure that customers come away from each, satisfied with the service. The points of contact are:

1    the visit to the cyberstore;

2    the point when they place their order;

3    the e-mail message that they get when their order has been received and is being processed, with a projected due date; and

4    the final delivery of their order.

Many catalog stores and cyberstores address the first three but few have gone to the pains that Bezos has gone to with the fourth. Amazon.com has created structures, literally, to ensure that customers are truly satisfied when their orders are received. Not only does this reduce returns but it also increases customer retention and loyalty, which, as Bezos has observed in interviews with the press, works for the organization because of the power of word-of-mouth on the web.

## ENSURE SAFE, SPEEDY DELIVERY

In Jeff Bezos' view, memorable service doesn't end until the product has been safely delivered. Whereas EDP acts as an effective, efficient linchpin between the site's order taking system and suppliers' inventory system – and thereby contributes to the service level consumers receive – Amazon.com's warehouse operations ensure not only speedy delivery but products which are well packaged and in good condition.

To appreciate the supply chain managed by Amazon.com, both the front end and back end of the cyberstore's business need to be studied in the light of traditional retail.

# AMAZON.COM'S
# COMPETITIVE EDGE

While business books reportedly aren't Bezos' favorite reading, no doubt he is familiar with Michael Porter's three strategies by which organizations achieve competitive advantage or have an edge over their corporate rivals. The choice should be based on the firm's strengths and its competitors' and prospective competitors' weaknesses. The secret of selection of strategy is choosing that strategy that plays to your firm's strengths where the competition isn't strong. Here are the three strategies:

◆ **Strategy #1: cost-leadership strategy.** Companies that pursue this strategy differentiate themselves on the basis of price. Porter has pointed to the fact that companies that follow this strategy have to be sure that they are always price leaders, offering the same quality as others for considerably less money. Cost advantage can come from any number of tactics, including technological innovations, low-cost labor, or economies of scale.

◆ **Strategy #2: customer differentiation strategy.** Companies choose this strategy if they believe that their organization can provide prospective customers with something that they deem important and others in the marketplace can't do the same. This, then, becomes the means by which these organizations differentiate themselves from rivals in their market. The differentiation may be a matter of quality or design, or convenience, or quality of service, expertise, or positive brand image. The secret to using this strategy, Porter has said, is to select a differentiator that is different from competitors' and would be important enough to customers to pay a premium price. So Mary Kay cosmetics have a unique distribution system, and L. L. Bean differentiates itself from other catalog clothing companies with extraordinary service, and

Armani is known as a prestige brand, and Maytag is remembered for the Maytag man (think "reliability").

◆ **Strategy #3: focus strategy.** This strategy takes one of the two earlier strategies and applies it to a niche within the market. So an example would be Lean Cuisine, the line of frozen dinners that offers a high-quality meal for calorie counters.

Amazon.com would seem to fall into this last category. Its niche is defined both by its product line and distribution channel – the web. Its differentiator is its focus on providing outstanding customer service. Like The Home Depot, the virtual store offers a broad selection of titles and demonstrates a commitment to service, qualities highly valued by customers. And the internal operations that allow it to pursue this strategy include its reliance on outside suppliers and own distribution network. (Incidentally, Amazon.com has built a similar network in Europe where it has two web sites, Amazon.co.uk and Amazon.de.) These external partners form a value-chain relationship that should have a positive impact on the company's continued growth, success, and ultimate ability to show a profit, something everyone outside of Amazon.com is awaiting with bated breath. Within the company, focus is on a belief held by Jeff Bezos and many money managers – and a friend of mine. That is, that the malls of today will disappear in a few years, becoming eye sores on the landscape.

# LOOK AT THE BIG PICTURE

The National Retail Federation suggests that the success of a retail operation depends on a number of factors, including:

1  parking facilities

2  demographics of local population

3   attractiveness of the storefront and layout of the building

4   proximity to a place of ongoing public interest

5   volume of traffic

6   safety and security of the area

7   ample product line

8   courtesy and knowledge of clerks

9   sufficient space for storage

10  inventory and quick availability of back order goods.

Interestingly, whereas the list of ten was developed for traditional retail businesses, they are also applicable to Amazon.com.
The firm doesn't need a parking lot, but it does need to be
accessible 24 hours a day to those who come to the site, and to
date, Amazon.com has been down only twice since it was
launched. Regarding demographics, Amazon is well suited to
the "local" population, albeit web surfers who tend to be technologically advanced, educated, and affluent consumers. It may
not be located on "Main and Main Street" or in some pricey
mall, but its offering of books, CDs, videos, and other entertaining, inspiring, or teaching products would seem to be well
suited to web traffic. Web page design and customized content
for frequent purchasers make for an attractive "storefront" and
additional editorial content in the form of reviews, interviews,
excerpts, and related recommendations make for deeper exploration of the site (think store "displays").

The web is expected to grow by 2003 percent over the next few years, which addresses the issue of proximity to a place of on-going public interest. Likewise, the volume of traffic is set to increase, as word-of-mouth over newsgroups and forums, and placement of banners and hotlinks at associate sites draw surfers to the Amazon store. Encryption using proprietary technology covers many of the issues of safety and security, but for those who are still wary about using their credit cards to buy goods, the virtual retailer offers more traditional ways to place orders. Variety and nature of merchandise have both grown and continue to outdistance any brick-and-mortar store. And while Amazon.com is saved the staffing expenses of clerks, it provides tremendous amounts of information for visitors about the products it offers, even information about shoddy merchandise in the form of negative reviews.

Finally, when we look at issues of storage, inventory and availability of goods we see that Amazon.com's unique supply-distribution network has enabled it to invest its money in enhancing brand, technological advancements, and storetainment (interesting and insightful editorial content).

## LOOK AT THE BIG PICTURE

Amazon.com is "virtual" not only in the absence of brick-and-mortar shopping outlets – the domain of traditional retailers who are moving online – but also in the way that it designates the maintenance of its own inventory to others. Consequently, storage space becomes a non-issue. Bezos' firm depends on wholesale distributors like Ingram, Baker & Taylor, and independent publishers and music and video companies for the stock it sells, thereby saving the organization a major cost allocation. As an article in *Wired* magazine suggested, these suppliers' own facilities serve as warehouses for Amazon.com. Since the company orders books and other products that customers have agreed to buy, the organization's return rate is said to be less than 0.25 percent compared to return numbers as high as 30 percent – the remainder rate in the book publishing industry. Product titles make up a digitized catalog, which, with Amazon.com editorial content, provides as much and often much more information than mail order catalog houses like Lillian Vernon, Harriet Carter, and Hanover Direct. On its site, Amazon.com has created one-stop shopping for a range of products that entertain, inspire, or teach, just as Toronto Dominion has made its Web site into a one-stop financial shopping center with information on savings plans, and other products and services it offers. But Toronto Dominion's site offers around 300 "pages" of content, whereas Amazon.com estimates its content as equivalent to 15 telephone directories for the biggest cities in the world. This approach to retail has been called "one of those ideas that are so inspired, you're amazed that no one thought of it sooner."

**Packaged with goods is a brochure that reads, "Discover books you'll love at Amazon.com"**

Unfortunately, there is one weakness with the idea: if the supply is cut off.

Currently, Ingram provides over 50 percent of Amazon.com's book titles, and Barnes and Noble, Amazon.com's chief competitor threatened to acquire it in 1999. Barnes and Noble and Ingram both promised that this purchase would not interfere with Amazon.com's relationship with Ingram, but it is understandable that Bezos is reportedly looking for alternative sources for books.

In the interim, as a digital business, dependent on others for just-as-needed delivery of titles, Amazon.com doesn't need much real estate. But that doesn't mean that it doesn't need any at all.

## SHIP ON TIME, GET ORDERS THERE SAFELY

There are five warehouses owned by Amazon.com, including one in Washington State, one in Delaware and one in Nevada. One is located in Seattle, another in New Castle in Delaware, and the latest, opened in early 1999, in Fernley, Nevada. An integral part of the firm's effort to enhance customers' experience, these state-of-the-art facilities maintain quality control over the packaging and shipping of products. With the company's data system, not only can orders from multiple publishers be shipped at one time but books can be packaged with CDs and/or videos also ordered. In the process, Amazon.com employees (called "associates" at the company) can check for defective goods, like cracked CD packaging.

Warehouses are located with purpose. For instance: Delaware, where the fledgling firm set up the second warehouse, does not have a sales tax. Nevada was chosen to speed delivery on the west coast. But there is another reason. Nevada is a tax-free state too, and Fernley is located near Reno, Nevada, close enough to the huge California population but just outside the state's tax-collection borders.

# ALIGN DISTRIBUTION WITH STRATEGIC PLANS

It should be clear that the distribution network was a key part of the plan that Bezos showed venture capitalists as he presented his dream of a virtual bookstore. The network that he has created achieves the following:

◆ Reflects an understanding of customers' delivery needs.

◆ Offers both current titles and hard-to-find editions and copies through the use of wholesale suppliers and independent producers.

◆ Provides two-day delivery on most orders through the Amazon warehousing setup.

◆ Enables customers – through EDI – to query the status of their purchases and track their own shipments.

◆ Aligns supply and delivery to other functions such as marketing, sales, and customer service.

There would seem to be no question that Jeff Bezos designed the business plan for Amazon.com around the fact that he would not need to stock titles in order to sell them, and consequently could save money which traditional retailers have to spend on brick-and-mortar outlets to increase their revenue streams. It has enabled him to focus on branding his site. Which is what he has told the press is one of his major concerns, along with continually satisfying his customers – which his supply-distribution network would seem ideally suited to do.

# CONTINUALLY REVISIT THE SYSTEM TO ENSURE THAT IT PROVIDES WHAT CUSTOMERS WANT

Under Campbell's old distribution system, goods sometimes arrived in poor condition at the warehouse. The shipping pallets weren't standardized, and consequently the company lost money on damaged goods. To solve the problem, Campbell's contracted with a rental company to provide standardized pallets for all deliveries. The firm not only reduced damage to goods but also increased the possible load on each truck. At Amazon.com, the value of handling final shipment and delivery of its products has prompted Bezos to increase the capacity and state-of-art of his warehouse facilities, and the number of such facilities and locations. Amazon.com may be able to reduce the costs of delivery if it can arrange for shipments directly to and from wholesalers and independent suppliers. Campbell's has done this with its Direct Plant Shipping program, which ships goods directly from specific plants to customers, bypassing the distribution center, and thereby making savings that are shared with the customers. Bezos sees the quality control function of the warehousing operation worth any additional operating costs.

## REDEFINING RETAIL

One of my friends does much of his shopping for house cleaning supplies, foodstuff, and paper products online. If Jeff Bezos is right, most of us will be doing the same by the year 2010. Some traditional stores will still exist but they will survive only because they do one of two things. Either they make the shopping experience fun, with a more personalized service, and also some form of entertainment, perhaps live music for adults and recreation for the kids. Or they offer 24-hour service and a broad enough range of necessities to allow us to rush out and pick up what we need, whether it's 2 p.m. or 2 a.m.

Among the online retailers that are proving this future more than a technological pipedream, Amazon.com offers the "world's largest selection" of items to entertain, inspire, and teach, and they are all available for purchase online.

# THE STARS IN BEZOS' DISTRIBUTION NETWORK

Based on the construction of his supply chain and interviews with the press, Jeff Bezos firmly believes that logistics:

◆ **Begin with the customer.** The business plan he first presented to venture capitalists demonstrated an understanding of web customers, and he continues to amass information on their wants and desires, no doubt, from information gathered at the web site, monitoring cyberbuzz, and focus groups. Whereas the initial plan was designed to allow him to sell books without the cost of brick-and-mortar buildings, Bezos had to be sure that the final setup would ensure titles available to customers, and prompt and safe shipments. Hence the recent addition of three warehouses to speed delivery.

◆ **Be alert to the various "moments of truth."** Each contact is critical to a satisfied customer. And this is a message that is communicated to all associates throughout Amazon.com.

◆ **Tie distribution logistics to marketing issues.** For instance, the decisions to locate warehouses in Delaware, and in a Nevada city just across the border from California, were well planned to reduce sales taxes on purchases. Maintenance of shipping within his own operation is also very much in keeping with the concern that has become almost a mantra at the company about the importance of servicing the customer.

◆ **Provide a single face to customers.** Yes, while titles come from various wholesalers and independent suppliers, it is to Amazon.com that we go to order our books and to make our other purchases. It is also from Amazon.com that we expect e-mail updates on progress on our orders, and from where our orders are shipped. It is to them that we can turn if problems arise.

# BIBLIOGRAPHY

Kuglin Fred A. (1998) *Customer-Centered Supply Chain Management*, Amacom, New York.

Bayers, Chip (1999) "Jeff Bezos – Why him (and not you)?" *Wired*, March.

Seven

# STAY LEAN

"Put your money where your need is."
**– Madeline E. Cohen, Staff Trainer, American Greetings Corporation Training & Development Journal**

Early business magazine stories about the launching of Amazon.com talk about a founder and chief executive officer whose desk is made from a door with four by fours for legs and whose associates' desks are similarly made; whose technology-based firm has the latest computers but whose monitors are propped up on stacks of telephone books; and whose offices have so few chairs that chairs for meetings are taken from those who leave them unguarded.

Further, the organization this CEO headed, while declaring itself the store of the future, operated out of a drab 1960s-style four-story building in Seattle. More, while this fledgling firm's CEO talked to reporters continuously about the importance of branding for his virtual organization, the company's headquarters, located above and behind a dry cleaners, had no sign marking its occupation of the building. Since then, the company has moved its headquarters three times, and now staff are spread out in four buildings in downtown Seattle, in addition to its Northwest warehouse location, in an industrial area near the port facilities. Before acquiring additional space, many offices were doubled or tripled up, including executive offices.

All this made for good editorial for an otherwise traditional startup business story, even the story of a virtual company on the Web. Those articles that didn't attribute the lean office furnishings and humble abode to a shortage of cash typical of an entrepreneurial firm or the virtual nature of its business, attributed it to the eccentricities of its CEO.

# SEE FRUGALITY AS A STRATEGIC NECESSITY

What's the truth? The management frugality practised by Amazon.com since its launch would seem a strategic necessity. Watching overhead enables the organization to spend more on branding and business expansion, allowing it to grow faster.

Much of the focus of discussion about the tight ship Bezos runs has focused on the surroundings, but the frugality has extended beyond office ambience. Amazon.com staff have been paid base salaries slightly less than competitive rates on average – competitive at the lowest levels of the organization and then increasingly behind the market at higher levels within the organization. The company also has no short-term incentive system, so total cash compensation has been slightly below competition. On the other hand, staff have shares in the public company that could make them considerably richer than their counterparts in other organizations when Amazon.com makes a profit.

However, staff are working for their riches. Although the number of employees has grown to over 1000 to date, the cyberstore still has fewer employees than offline organizations and even other e-tailers doing similar business volume. So employees put in long and hard days.

# WORK HARD, HAVE FUN, MAKE HISTORY

The company's management offers employees the opportunity to make history by helping to make the cyberstore a success – the company sees itself out to change both how people shop and how they think about shopping. Its management promises that the effort will be fun, but it also warns that it will be hard work. A recruitment brochure from Amazon.com warns, "We're demanding of our employees, so we look for people who are demanding of themselves." "Were the Crusades a nine-to-five job?" a research report for job seekers published by Web Feet asks. "Amazon.com isn't, either." Clearly, so long as Amazon.com continues in its investment phase, in which rapid growth is expected to be accomplished with thin staffing, employees who aren't willing to work long hours or take responsibility beyond their job titles, aren't likely to fit in.

## LIVE THE MESSAGE

Until recently, this lean approach even extended into Bezos' personal life. In the first few years after the site's launch, there was considerable fun made about Bezos' lifestyle in discussion groups and chat rooms on the Web. Specifically, the talk was about the one-bedroom rental in downtown Seattle, ten blocks from the office, where Bezos lived with his wife Mackenzie, and his dog Tamala. Although a multimillionaire from his share of Amazon.com, Bezos reportedly still drove his wife's Honda until recently. While Bezos' lifestyle would now seems more typical of other high-tech entrepreneurs –

WebFeet.com, an information resource for job seekers, advises about Amazon.com, "Amazon.com management is evangelical about Amazon's mission, and if you want to be successful there it will help if you, too, can take up the crusade."

he's bought a mansion – he is likely to continue to promote frugality at Amazon.com. True, the organization is consolidating all but warehousing operations in the Pacific Medical Building in Seattle, and there will be comparatively more spacious and palatial facilities, but as a retailer, albeit one not of bricks and mortar, razor-thin margins will likely be a way of life.

## PRACTISE FRUGALITY AS A VALUE

Frugality is a value at Amazon.com. What's a value? A value is like a goal in that it is an ongoing objective, but it is more. It is a force or ideal, or philosophy at the center of the organization whose practice can often determine the difference between success and failure of the enterprise. At Amazon.com, a lean operation is necessary to allow the organization to continue to invest, to grow site traffic.

## PUT MONEY WHERE IT'S NEEDED

In order to get people to its site, Amazon.com has spent considerably to get its name into the marketplace and build brand awareness. This money has gone into several initiatives, including:

◆ building partnerships with search engines like Yahoo!

◆ purchasing banners on portals like AOL

◆ paying participants in its Associates Program

◆ creating a variety of offline promotional activities

◆ continuing innovation on the site itself

◆ staying ahead of the technology curve.

---

## LEAN MANAGEMENT TO SUSTAIN SUCCESS

As past economic downturns have demonstrated, there are management benefits in keeping a company from growing fat. As companies grow quickly, as Amazon.com has done, the expansion can undermine financial controls and threaten long-term success unless management promulgates the need for operating efficiencies. A case in point is CompUSA, one of the fastest-growing retailers in the early 1990s, whose survival was endangered as rapid growth outstripped systems in place and weakened the chain's balance sheet.

The company's leadership needed to be changed.

Jeff Bezos runs a tight ship, not only because he needs the money to spend to promote the site and keep visitors coming to his cyberstore, but also because he is well aware that lean companies are better able to change and reinvent themselves as fast as market changes demand and can compete on price as well as customer service. Lean management doesn't have to equate with mean management, either; working for an enterprise that practises frugality can be fun, as insiders at Amazon.com attest in interviews.

The goal is to have a store that people want to revisit time and time again. Since Amazon.com doesn't have a sales clerk at your shoulder to lead you through the cyberstore, it has to use technology to simulate, and improve on, the experience. As such, frugality is the base of a pyramid of values. From frugal management, there will be money available to accomplish the other values critical to the organization's success:

◆ satisfied customers

◆ ever-increasing traffic to the site through strategic alliances

◆ product extensions, and new service offerings

◆ brand enhancement to differentiate Amazon.com from both brick-and-mortar retailers and e-competitors.

The last comes from servicing customers at or beyond their expectations. Land's End is its own brand. The Container Store is a brick-and-mortar store, but it is also a brand. Amazon.com, too, is a brand built on the quality of its service.

## SPOTLIGHT VALUES

The need to run a tight ship is a message that is repeated to employees and staff by Bezos and his top management team, along with the message about customer satisfaction and brand enhancement and innovation. There are various ways that executives lead their organization. Repetition of corporate values is one. Leadership is the ability to make things happen, and leaders do this by identifying opportunities for growth and pursuing them. They act as a catalyst for continuous operational improvements, encouraging and channeling the contributions of others by being clear about the values important to the organization. Bezos has told the press and his employees that the issue right now isn't Amazon.com's profitability but it's growth. Staff are asked not to watch stock prices but rather look to the needs of customers since satisfaction of their expectations will determine the ultimate success of Amazon.com and its stocks. The focus is on the customer.

If it's good for him or her, it's worth doing.

> **"Bezos projects the egalitarianism of the place," an insider reportedly said.**

Bezos knows that customer expectations grow as the bar is raised. This is true in real-time business and it is equally true on the Web. If anything, expectations about e-tailers change more rapidly than expectations about retailers because of the different timeframes in which they operate.

While leaders' personalities may differ, there are several characteristics that they have in common. Jeff Bezos, like other great business leaders, knows how important it is to:

◆ Stand firm when necessary. Which is what he would seem to be doing when it comes to the investment phase of Amazon.com's growth. Money is a resource, like time and people, to be invested as external and internal conditions demand.

◆ Openly acknowledge that your stand may not be popular with all but then explain why it is important to the organization's success. If lean staff or operating conditions are needed, be courageous in pursuing this stand.

◆ Translate this value into specific behaviors and communicate these to your senior staff. In turn, have your top managers communicate behaviors to the next level below. And so on. Values must be translated into behaviors to enable employees to better understand how their actions can affect the enterprise's ultimate success.

If frugality is important to your organization's success either over the short-term or long-term, maybe for perpetuity, be sure

# VALUES-DRIVEN ORGANIZATIONS

Whatever the corporate values, they can move employees to make decisions and direct their actions as their organization – regardless if virtual or real time – wishes. Values unite employees under common objectives. Jeff Bezos has built his organization around the primary value of customer satisfaction and, toward achievement of that value, the secondary value of operational frugality to have the funds to both enhance brand and acquire other businesses in order to encourage visitors to the cyberstore.

Regardless of the business you build, values are equivalent to corporate goals, set to ensure the firm's achievement of its strategy. There's much written about the use of corporate values for achieving performance excellence and corporate competitive advantage, but frequently there are gaps between the values promulgated by management and the values practised. Further, employees have no clear-cut direction about the behaviors that the values demand. If an organization is to use values to spur employee and corporate performance, then its management needs to do the following:

◆ **Be clear about why the values are important.** Early in the history of Amazon.com, Jeff Bezos reportedly met with staff at his fledgling company every three months to remind them to place attention, not on the value per share of Amazon.com stock they held, but the importance of continuous outstanding service to the organization's ultimate success. Successful values-driven organizations know that employees who have no idea of the importance of values won't work hard to achieve them. They likely won't care until management explains to them how they are tied to the company's competitive position and/or market strategy.

◆ **Translate the values into job performance.** Senior management needs to relate values or corporate goals to employee responsibilities. Telling an employee about a value, whether it's customer service, frugality, or high productivity, means little unless it is translated into activities or behaviors that employees can follow.

◆ **Prioritize the values.** Unless management makes clear those activities that are tied to important values and that therefore have greater priority, those activities may not be done first. Here's where gaps between values promulgated and those practised can be confusing.

◆ **Provide positive consequences** for employees who pursue the values. Needless to say, when Amazon.com begins to show a profit, its employees who all hold stock shares, will profit too. But regardless of the incentive, whether financial or not, there should be acknowledgment that the individual supported the corporate value. It can be lunch for two or a plaque, but it should send the message, "You did well." Behaviors won't change if employees don't see a benefit – some payoff.

◆ **Role model the values.** This is important for senior management. If the employee doesn't see anyone but himself or herself practicing the espoused values, then the employee is more likely to see himself or herself as a chump rather than a hero or heroine.

that potential employees understand that reality. Otherwise, turnover can be fierce. In Bezos' case, he has been able to bring to his organization not only very creative individuals for whom the challenge is extremely important but talented individuals who believe as much as he does in the broader objective of Amazon.com. Web Feet Publishing's research report on Amazon.com compares the enthusiasm of Amazon.com's employees to the evangelical fervor of the Crusaders.

## BALANCE THE BAD WITH THE GOOD

The challenge to work at what could be an entirely new way of doing business is part of what keeps employees at Amazon.com. But there are other values than frugality, and any discussion of the values promulgated by Bezos should mention those as well. You can run a tight ship but it helps to balance frugality with other values to make the long hours and hard work emotionally rewarding. In earlier chapters, we have discussed the importance placed on innovation and customer service and, yes, these would seem to be values at Amazon.com. But stories in the press in which insiders are interviewed suggest that employees have much autonomy in their job. Which can offset the lack of a real desk. There's a sense of teamwork and trust, too, something many employees in today's fat-cat organizations would argue don't exist. "It's a very open environment and employees seem willing to help each other," one Amazon.com insider reportedly said. The firm seems to be a collaborative, team-based organization with minimal hierarchy. Bezos himself is known to be personable and accessible to staff. And, maybe most important, as he asks for frugality from staff, he also practises it. He doesn't have a ritzy corner office or a $2000

# CORPORATE FOLKLORE

The histories of start-ups are filled with stories that grow in the telling. Over time, as the founding of the company takes on heroic qualities, these tales become the folklore of the business. Nowhere more so than in the start-up of one of the most successful cyberstores on the Web. The story has made Bezos' departure from his previous employer to start his own firm seem more like a mythological quest than a logical business decision based on a careful study of the Web, a business plan based on supply-chain management that would work nowhere but on the Internet, and the entrepreneurial spirit of a Bill Gates or a Michael Dell. It doesn't matter how true the story of Bezos' drive from the east to west coast is. It has become corporate folklore, and in turn it has created a corporate culture that has created a sense of community in those who work at the company. The shared history and sense of belonging have made it easier to get support for the values deemed critical to Amazon.com's success: frugality, customer satisfaction, and continuous growth through brand enhancement, acquisition, and strategic alliance.

desk – he has one of those $130 jerry-built desks made out of a door.

# THE SECRET OF A
# SUCCESSFUL START-UP

Any entrepreneur will tell you that cashflow is an issue of major concern over the first few years with a start-up. Never more so in e-commerce where the secret is to get as many visitors to the cyberstore as possible. It's this that has made maintaining a lean operation critical to Amazon.com.

Frugality is a value at Amazon.com, and Bezos:

◆ Role models it himself. There is no fancy office for him, any more than there are for his senior staff or other employees. If you want to see a value practised, you practise it yourself.

◆ Talks the talk as well as walks the talk. Regularly Bezos is said to meet with staff to remind them of key issues in the organization's success. Customer satisfaction is one. Continuous reinvention is another. Trust and teamwork are critical. But so is keeping staff numbers to a minimum and doing without fancy office furnishings.

◆ Sends a clear message to staff that they have to do more than pull their own weight. That message is: "Work hard, have fun, make history." Because his employees believe that they, indeed, are making history working for one of the most popular cyberstores on the Web, they are willing to put in those long hours. The fun part comes from knowing that they have lots of autonomy and can take reasonable risks so long as it satisfies the customer.

# UNDERSTANDING AMAZON

When we look at Amazon.com's Web site, we have to realize that we are seeing the end result of the work of three distinct groups:

◆ The product development group – concerned with editorial, marketing, site design, and site navigation.

◆ The software development group – information technology systems (fulfillment, distribution center software, as well as finance and HR software) and the Web site software group. In addition, there's the system network and operation center (or SNOC), which is responsible for information technology, systems maintenance and implementation of new software tools. The IT and SNOC groups report to the CIO; Web site and software engineering report to the vice president of engineering.

◆ Supply chain and distribution management, which includes the company's distribution network and which reports to the chief logistics officer. Under this group is also customer service.

# BIBLIOGRAPHY

Anonymous (1998) "Amazon.com: the wild world of e-commerce," *BusinessWeek,* December 14.

Hazleton, Lesley (1998) "Jeff Bezos: how he built a billion-dollar net worth for his company even before his company turned a profit," *Success,* July.

*Amazon.com: The Online Jungle and More, The Company Insider.* Published by Wetfeet Press, The Information Resource for Job Seekers, San Francisco, California.

Eight

# PRACTISE TECHNOLEVERAGE

"The nerds have won."
**– Tom Peters**

Amazon.com is a retail company, but it is also a technology company. And it is that which has made Amazon a leader in e-commerce. Technology:

◆ Drives opportunities, helping organizations gain short-term advantage and position themselves for longer-term success.

◆ Enables start-ups to outperform established businesses by finding new and better ways of servicing the same marketplace.

◆ Positions an organization with a great idea to move beyond its initial marketplace or product line to expand its customer base.

On the Web, it also enables a company to do business that it might not otherwise be able to do, as is the case with Amazon.com. One of the most popular cyberstores on the Web would not be able to compete with established brick-and-mortar stores if it didn't have a virtual inventory available through a network of wholesalers and independent producers, linked to its site by EDI.

## PURCHASE IF YOU CAN, DEVELOP IF YOU MUST

Amazon.com was launched with its own software, developed by Bezos and his first employees in his garage. Bezos told the press that the toughest part of being a start-up electronic merchant in 1994 was that there were no off-the-shelf software tools that would enable his firm to secure credit card orders or confirm purchases via e-mail. He expected that situation to change, and advised e-retailers that came after his firm to buy ready-made programs. But to start his firm he had to build his own, utilizing the best programmers he could hire.

> Robert D. Hof of *BusinessWeek* says Amazon was the first commercial site to use "collaborative filtering" technologies to analyze customer purchases and suggest other books that people with similar purchase histories like.

Linking the Web site's network – a Unix-based, 10Base-T configuration, with Digital Equipment alpha servers – to book wholesalers was EDI. As orders were placed, Amazon.com used EDI to contact book distributors to check title availability. Order information was sent via EDI rather than via IP-based programs because major book suppliers Ingram, and Baker & Taylor used it. But it was more than that. Bezos said that it was the safest, fastest way to handle huge inventories.

## SUSTAIN YOUR COMPANY'S LEADERSHIP ROLE

Developments since then include proprietary technology, 1-Click™ ordering, to streamline the ordering process, a state-of-the-art recommendation center, numerous subject browsing areas for book, music, or video buyers, and much, much more to increase the benefits of online shopping and strengthen the company's position in e-commerce.

There are five distribution centers. In August 1998, Amazon.com purchased two companies: Junglee Corp., which has developed comparison-shopping technologies; and PlanetAll, which is an Internet site that helps people stay in touch with friends. PlanetAll could evolve into a reminder service for Amazon to prompt customers to buy Amazon products for friends and family members. Which excites Bezos. "PlanetAll is the most innovative use of the Internet I've seen," he said. "It's simply a breakthrough in doing something as fundamental and important as staying in touch. The reason PlanetAll has over 1.5 million members – and is growing even faster than the Internet – is simple. It creates extraordinary value for its users. I believe that PlanetAll will prove to be one of the most important online applications."

## ACQUIRE TECHNOLOGY

If Bezos is excited about PlanetAll, money managers are even more enthusiastic about the implications of Junglee in Bezos' hands. Despite his protests that he isn't interested in his site becoming a portal – in press meetings he contends it is a destination site – money managers talk about the likelihood of its moving Amazon.com into an Internet shopping portal or go-through site that consumers can use to purchase products that Amazon doesn't sell directly. Junglee Corp.'s technology is currently used by shoppers on America Online and Yahoo!, which would prompt these portals to license the technology's use from Amazon.com. Is this move likely? Bezos' response is to remind corporate crystal gazers that Amazon has numerous deals with the big portals and that it gets its exposure through them. He would not want to jeopardize these partnerships, which, market analysts say, played a big part in Amazon.com's early success and continued traffic. Amazon.com, Bezos has told the press, is a go-to site, another term he uses for destination site, and its branding strategy is designed to ensure anyone on the Web who keys in the words "Amazon.com" gets immediately to his store.

# RAISE THE TECHNOLOGICAL BAR

While Bezos apparently disagrees with money managers on this issue, he agrees that his company is a technology firm first and a retailer second. From the beginning, Bezos has used the power of technology, firstly to compete successfully against brick-and-mortar retailers and, now, to outperform many of those same retailers who have chosen to expand online to compete on Bezos' grounds. Which won't be easy. When Bezos launched Amazon, it was state of the art, yet it was, in his opinion, only one-tenth as good as it is today. The technological bar is forever being raised. Beyond that, start-ups that learned retail in brick-and-mortar stores will be competing with someone who knew the Web even before he launched his company. In the interim he has learned much more about cybershoppers, including why many shop on the Web and many others still don't, and what can be done technologically to encourage more to make their purchases from their office chair or home armchair.

Little known is the fact that before Amazon.com, Bezos founded a company to build intranets for businesses with the goal of delivering personalized news to stockholders. The year was 1989, and his partner was Halsey Minor, founder and CEO of the online news service C/NET. The firm folded when financing dried up due to the great downsizing of 1990.

# COMPENSATE FOR SYSTEMS SHORTCOMINGS

Although he sees tremendous potential in the Web, the underlying technology is still in its infancy. For instance, it still takes consumers 60 seconds to boot up. "A bootup of 60 seconds is unacceptable to most people," he told *Upside* magazine. "Wait for an elevator for 60 seconds and see how you feel about it." Browsers crash and call waiting interrupts connections. So online sellers have to offer "an overwhelming value proposition" to compensate. Which is clearly what Amazon is doing. To compensate for technological shortcomings, Bezos explains, he discounts products, offers a huge selection of products – many of which can't be found elsewhere – provides personalization, and offers instant recommendations. A successful online retailer must add enough value to encourage potential customers to try a new way of shopping. "Buying habits are difficult to change," he says. "Focus on the value proposition, and make sure that the value proposition is incredibly high relative to the traditional way of doing business," he advises. "That's important right now because the Web is still a primitive technological platform with lots of inconveniences associated with using it for the customer."

# WHY BE A FOLLOWER IF YOU CAN BE LEADER?

A basic requirement of any firm on the Internet is that technologically it is state-of-the-art. But to surpass rivals, it must do even more, and always be at the cutting edge. Toward that, as Jeff Bezos demonstrates, you have to:

◆ **Conduct technology assessments** to identify technological needs of the market and organization. Such assessment identifies not only the nature of the technology but also its impact both on operating processes *and* strategic plans. For instance, if you set up a Web site, you might want to maintain a watch over the strategic technological development of your organization by closely monitoring, on a monthly basis, all projects within the organization that would advance existing technology or create a new technology. Certainly, Bezos, given his own technological bent, has maintained a focus on technological developments both on his Web site and back-end processes.

◆ **Be willing to invest in new technology.** It's cheaper and faster to buy ready-made software, and when you can get proprietary use of it, that may be better. However, to succeed in cyberspace, it is imperative that companies meet customer expectations, and expect them to be ever growing.

◆ **Always set the example.** If you are to get into the business of running a Web site, then you want your site to be the one to which customers compare existing and new businesses. Keep in mind that it isn't necessary to make giant leaps; even incremental improvements can impact customer impressions of your site. Consider how Amazon.com continues to meet customer expectations, not only in product offerings but technological capability.

◆ **Conduct frequent technology audits** to determine how your site stands up to competitors. Don't get so wound up running the business that you don't surf the Web yourself and monitor the newest services of other cyberstores via technological improvements. Consider the technology behind these services and its application to your business. If you are to be a frontrunner, if not leader of the pack as Amazon.com currently is, the technology evident in your site is as important as the appearance and products on sale there.

◆ **Acquire proprietary technology.** Bezos bought both Junglee and PlanetAll, thereby buying technology that down the road will have a significant impact on the success of his cyberstore, whatever it ultimately becomes. In the meantime, purchase of the technology has added to the cyberbuzz on the Web and consequently is likely to draw prospective customers to the site to test out the latest offering. Likewise, his most recent move to run auctions from the site.

◆ **Overcome technological shortcomings.** Give visitors to your site reason to wait for the site to boot up, like interesting editorial content or fun ways to get involved, including giving amateur authors the opportunity to complete a chapter of a book by a best-selling author. And give those still wary about buying off the Web sufficient reassurances and, if they still aren't convinced, alternative ways to purchase.

◆ **Be flexible in your strategy.** New technology can change organization tactics, even shift strategy. Technoleverage requires not only maximizing the newest technology available but also adapting, where appropriate, organizational plans and strategies, as well as processes, to reflect the technological changes. Whether you develop or purchase the technoleverage to add competitive advantage, you have to assess its impact on the longer term as well as short term.

# OFFER REASSURANCES TO THE WARY

For one, consumers are still wary about purchasing over the Internet if it requires them to give their credit card numbers. At Amazon.com, that concern has receded, owing to the many reassurances, and alternatives on offer. If customers wish, they can use the Netscape Secure Commerce Server, which encrypts the information so that it can't be read in transit. Others pay by check, while still others will place their orders online, entering only the last five digits of their card number, then phoning in the rest. When Amazon.com was first launched, half of its customers called in their card numbers; today that figure is down to as low as 5 percent. This may, in part, be due to another technological advance at Amazon. After a first purchase, customers' shipping and credit card information are stored securely so all it takes thereafter is a single click to send books to them. And orders are often upgraded to priority shipping for free.

# AVOID ME-TOO APPEARANCES

Newer online retailers imitate the look of Amazon.com, and many have offerings very similar to Amazon.com. Online shoppers point to BarnesandNoble.com's increasing visual similarity to Amazon.com and some small services it offers that Amazon.com doesn't, like a willingness to contact used-book sellers for difficult to find titles and discount periodical subscriptions. But they still see BarnesandNoble.com site as a "me-too," without the sense of community that Amazon.com's site offers with its reviews, interviews, first-view chapters of best-selling books, and other "fun" elements. So visitors to Amazon.com still outnumber its major competitors. Generally, when the gap closes between Bezos and his chief competitors, Bezos counteracts either by upgrading the technology or the offerings. The decision to purchase a minority share in online Drugstore.com was very likely prompted in part by statistics that showed visitors to BarnesandNoble.com doubled from September through November 1998 whereas Amazon.com only experienced a 40 percent increase. Stiff competition from Barnes and Noble and Border may also explain Amazon.com's reason to run auctions on its site.

> Bezos told *Forbes,* "Amazon.com is in every way a technology firm, and there are no sustainable technological advantages. If you use superior technology to differentiate yourself, it has to be an ongoing strategy."

As you will see in Chapter 10, the pressures being put on Bezos from competitors, direct and indirect, are considerable. As we have seen, Amazon's principal foe, Barnes and Noble, threatened to buy the Ingram Book Group, the largest US wholesaler to book retailers, including Amazon, and it sold 50 percent of its Web operations to publisher Bertelsmann AG, thereby gaining a potent competitive advantage. Further, nine major Web retailers, including eToys and CDnow, joined together in an online mall – Shopper Connection – to better compete against Amazon. And, finally, Wal-Mart, the country's largest retailer, launched its own Web site (www.wal-mart.com).

Amazon.com responded to Barnes and Noble's threat to acquire Ingram Book Group by reassuring investors that it would continue to diversify its supplier base. And it added a link to

Drugstore.com on its site, giving online purchasers another reason to visit in response to the closing gap between it and BarnesandNoble.com, the recent launch of Wal-Mart online, and the alliance of nine. It would seem like a business version of a Nintendo game if the stakes weren't so high. Certainly one move in the game is always to make usage of Amazon.com easier than any of the competition, via technology.

## BE OPEN TO FUTURE OPPORTUNITIES

There are technological opportunities that Bezos may have on a to-do list he has yet to take action on. Asked, for instance, about the possibility of electronic distribution of books, he has answered "yes." Is it something for the immediate future? "No," Bezos says, but he doesn't discount the possibility. Just the opposite. He says, "It is not a question of if, it's a question of when. The reason it's slow to happen is because the display technology has not yet caught up with paper. That's not good yet for the end customer. That will get fixed over time, as display technology gets better."

## UNDERSTAND E-COMMERCE

The timeframe for such a development could be one week on the Internet, according to Robert Baldock, of Andersen Consulting. A year could be 35 calendar days, a reflection of online innovation. E-commerce, he continues, is taking off, observing that Dell Computer sells $1 million worth of PCs on the Internet every day, and anticipates an increase to an annual $1 billion by the year 2000. Whereas today there are still consumers uneasy about buying on the Web using a credit card, estimates suggest electronic commerce will reach $200 to $300 billion by 2001. By that year, over 300 million consumers from around the world will be connected to the Internet, providing a huge potential for retailers. A survey by Master Card for the National Retail Federation found out why. Consumers will turn more and more to electronic shopping due to:

1   increasing dissatisfaction with traditional store shopping, with its poor service, lack of product knowledge, and variety

2   decreasing fear of computers

3   the booming number of e-retailers.

Bezos offers deep price discounts for his products, but he does not believe they bring consumers to his site, and he is likely right. The survey found abundant product information so pleased consumers that they were willing to pay a little more, particularly given the convenience and speed of electronic shopping.

# INTEGRATE THE TECHNOLOGY INTO ALL ORGANIZATIONAL FUNCTIONS

While much of the focus of discussion about technology is on the Web site, equally state-of-the-art are the US-based warehouses operated by Amazon.com from which purchases from wholesalers and independent producers are shipped directly to consumers. Each of these facilities have the latest packaging and warehousing technology to speed delivery.

They are part of an overall technological strategy designed to better service customers. Manufacturers have always used technology to build relationships with their customers. IBM took on Fujitsu and NEC by providing consultation on customers' data processing problems. Lincoln Electric Company trained its sales force so it could identify welding-related cost savings for customers. Bethlehem Steel moved its engineers out of its factories and put them in district sales offices to build closer customer ties. Likewise, there are opportunities for service organizations, whether it is variety of product, service offerings, ease of ordering or speedy delivery of the service. Amazon.com's technological strategy is designed to improve customer relations on both the front end and back end. Ease of usage is part of the story but there is also speedy communication to wholesalers and independent producers about products not readily available in the store's own warehouses. On the back end, money has been invested to provide quick and safe delivery of orders.

## LOOKING TOWARD THE FUTURE

In the months – and years – ahead, Bezos can expect more competition on the Internet. Upstarts have been known to take on established firms and overpower them, but then giants use their resources to retrieve their lost market share. An offline case in point is Virgin Cola, which tried to take on cola giants Pepsi and Coke in the UK, earned 4.7 percent market share, and then rapidly lost it when the giants consolidated their distribution and fought back with special promotions. An online example: when Netscape launched its browser on the Internet in October 1994, it went from nothing to 90 percent of the market in two years. Three years later, its market share had tumbled to 58 percent; Microsoft had packaged its own Internet browser as a free "extra" with its Windows operating system, thereby gaining 39 percent of market share.

In business, online and off, industry newcomers can become worldwide players overnight. Which is what has happened to Amazon online. But Bezos' firm could lose its position as a top cyberspace store if he doesn't continue to use the technological knowledge he has applied over the last four years. This can be summarized in the following key points:

> Anna C. Semansky suggests that "Amazon.com may be trying to reduce its dependency on portal traffic" with purchase of PlanetAll.

◆ Use technology to solve real problems. This is particularly true for start-up retailers that can't waste cash for technology for technology's sake. In Amazon's case, technology has been used for easy ordering, securing customer credit card numbers, and speeding delivery.

◆ Build on these basics, differentiating the site in order to build a high-growth business. Bezos did this by using market focus groups to better understand those extras that customers would appreciate, from online personalizations, to e-mail confirmations, to free priority mail for repeat customers.

◆ Invest consistently to enhance technological strengths. So Bezos purchased PlanetAll and Junglee. And expanded the navigational tools on the retail site.

◆ Search widely for new markets that value their capabilities. For Amazon.com, after it had established itself as the largest bookstore on the Web, it extended its product line to music and videos. In the beginning of 1999, the firm added pharmaceuticals through a hotlink to Drugstore.com. Then came the pet supplies and now groceries. And more are likely planned. Not only would these markets value the technological applications but the markets themselves have high profitability. Organizations that leverage technology are smart about getting out of or avoiding situations where they provide no unique high-value capability or where pricing is determined by others.

◆ Fully exploit an opportunity and overwhelm potential competitive firms. A case in point is customers' desire to make purchasing as easy as possible on the Web. Amazon.com maintains records of customer preferences and then acts on that information.

◆ Whatever the need you are addressing, address it as fully as you can. Gaps are opening for competitors to enter. Gaps stem from rushing to release a technological advance before it's perfected. So don't.

◆ Remember that what one programmer can create, another can copy, so keep innovating. Technology is a tool; a means to an end rather than the end itself. Try one approach; if that fails, try another, to the point of solution.

Continuous improvement isn't limited to technology, however. As the next chapter illustrates, one secret to Amazon's success is its ability to innovate.

## THE WEB BUSINESS

When Jeff Bezos presented his business plan to venture capitalists, he was able to tell them that, thanks to the Web, he could change the economics of the book industry as a whole. It took out-of-box thinking to use the Web to enter a market with established book chains and scramble the competition. Bezos did it, and the reader of this book can do the same in another market. Keep in mind that Bezos identified 20 products that, in his opinion, he could sell on the Web, likely using very much the same virtual logistics, with inventory maintained by wholesalers and other independents. In this economic model, remember that the biggest business right now isn't necessarily going to continue to be the leader if you understand e-commerce. In gatherings of book publishers, it is amazing how investor discussion invariably leads to discussion of Amazon.com and the "how come" question. *How come* it took someone outside the industry to see the opportunity of selling books on the Web? Becoming another Bezos on the Web lies in discovering a market others can't see – or think is seemingly too small or too unattractive to pursue – but could be mined on the Web.

## BIBLIOGRAPHY

Baldock, Robert (1999) *Destination Z: The History of the Future*, John Wiley & Sons, New York.

Doler, Kathleen (1998) "Interview: Jeff Bezos: founder and CEO of Amazon.com Inc." *Upside,* September.

Anonymous (1998) "Jeff Bezos: selling books, running hard!" April.

Anonymous (1998) "The river wild: Amazon.com's recent acquisitions move it into new territory," *Red Herring Magazine,* November.

Hof, Robert D. (1998) "technology, technology, technology" *BusinessWeek,* December 14.

Nine

# INNOVATION AND ENLIGHTENED ADAPTATION

"To stay ahead, you must have your next idea waiting in the wings."

**– Rosabeth Moss Kanter**

What makes for an innovative company? It's one that identifies customer needs today and also works to predict their needs in the future. Further, to satisfy today's needs, an innovative firm identifies other firms' best practices and adapts them to its own business needs. To address tomorrow's needs, it goes further, building new systems based on today's best practices.

Winning in business today needs this kind of daily reinvention. Just as having a strategic focus is essential to long-term success, being blind to marketplace changes is a derailing of success over the short term and profitability over the longer term. The pace of change accelerates in every industry, not solely in technologies, and companies must be alert to opportunities for new markets for existing products and new products in existing markets and, finally, new products for new markets. How do you do ensure this corporate-wide? An example: Rubbermaid has set a corporate goal to enter a new product category each and every year and to have one third of revenues stem from new products developed over the past five years. To ensure that best practices get shared throughout larger organizations, firms like Coca-Cola and BellSouth have created the role of chief learning officer, many of whom report directly to the chief executive officer. At Sears, the firm's chief administrative officer fulfills the role, responsible for Sears' culture of continuous learning (think "continuous improvement") based on customer feedback.

## GROWTH VS. STAGNATION

Monitoring the latest customer definition of "satisfaction" is the growth driver of successful entrepreneurial firms. Thriving firms – online and off – are those that are watchful of developments outside their organization – opportunities (customer choices, needs, and preferences) *and* challenges (competitor strategies and tactics) – and they make strategic decisions based on what they see. They reinvent themselves to cope with the environmental change – even rethink their mission as a company in volatile markets, as Amazon.com has done on the rapidly changing Internet – whereas stalled companies seem oblivious to both kinds of changes. Elliott Goodwin, president of Larry's Shoes in Fort Worth, Texas, blamed himself for a severe decline in corporate sales in the late 1980s. Focused on the wholesale side, dealing with vendors who each promised the hottest shoe fashion, he said he began to dictate to the stores what they should sell, oblivious to what local markets wanted. This created a store-versus-corporate environment and a deterioration in morale.

## ONE GOOD IDEA ISN'T ENOUGH

No one could say that Jeff Bezos is oblivious to external developments. Consequently his company is experiencing significant growth. Jeff Bezos runs an innovative organization and is, himself, a successful innovator. He recognizes that launching an organization, even one on the cutting edge such as Amazon.com, isn't enough. Thereafter, there must be a commitment to continuous improvement in systems, and quantum leaps in performance defined in terms of customer satisfaction. An example of the importance of the latter in the retail industry can be found in Wal-Mart's mission statement: "to provide a range of products that deliver value to Middle America."

Amazon.com may be online, but it is a retailer and consequently it is imperative that it delivers value to its customers. Which means efficient and effective inventory management and distribution networks and, most important, satisfied customers.

However, there's no question that in launching Amazon.com on the Web, Bezos has redefined retail; in making it one of the top cyberstores on the Web, he has also changed people's perceptions of e-commerce. One marketing expert has said about Amazon.com, that it "is an example of how an upstart can redefine its whole industry." In retail, it is often a matter of location, location, location, and Amazon.com's fortune on the Web has caused traditional retailers to scramble to join them. Not only did Bezos force brick-and-mortar book retail competitors Barnes and Noble and Border to set up sites on the Internet, but his success has prompted other brick-and-mortar retail giants, including Wal-Mart, to go online sooner than they might have planned.

*Business Week* observed: 'What Bezos understood before most people was that the ability of the Web to connect almost anyone with almost any product meant that he could do things that couldn't be done in the physical world – such as sell 3 million books in a single store."

Amazon's early success has also given real-time retailers reason to question whether traditional competitive advantages stand up today. Amazon.com has drawn sales from them through being the "largest inventory of books on the planet," offering "a unique shopping experience," and creating value-added offerings like book reviews, interviews, and excerpts of soon-to-be released best-sellers. Bookstores have responded by increasing their number of author readings and signings, providing reading alcoves for customers, and even setting aside valuable retail space for coffee bars.

In terms of the retail industry as a whole, Bezos has done what Wal-Mart did a decade or so ago. Wal-Mart programmed computers to track customer orders and built a network of distribution centers so it could replenish 85 percent of its vast product line in its stores within two days, compared to 65 percent of merchandise in five days or more of other retailers with smaller product lines. Bezos has used the Internet to offer a rich selection of products (in books alone, his inventory represents 15 times the size of any bookstore) and to provide personalized service for millions of customers.

# MEASURES OF PRODUCT WORTH

The changes Bezos has made in retailing have also led to changes for producers of the products he sells – in particular, the book industry, where sales data now maintained and reported on the Amazon.com site enables publishers to make tough decisions about what to publish and how many copies to produce. Through the Web, he has also given publishers a healthy new distribution channel – and not only the major publishers.

In February 1998, Amazon.com launched its Advantage program for smaller book publishers. Such publishers have had a problem getting into traditional distribution channels. Sales of a book must reach a certain number before it makes it into existing wholesale channels. A press release from Amazon.com suggested that the program would "help level the playing field for smaller publishers by providing the tools and framework to ensure their books appear more often and more prominently throughout Amazon.com's catalog of 2.5 million titles." Amazon.com would keep a limited quantity of member copies of books in its distribution centers for immediate availability, which would mean that these books could be shipped in 24 hours instead of four to six weeks, often the case for titles from independent publishers. Since these publishers might lack the funds to promote their books on the site, Amazon.com would offer free scans of independent publishers' book jackets, and help members in the program add title information such as descriptions, excerpts, tables of contents, and author and publisher comments.

Why did Amazon.com do this? Not only does the program enhance Amazon.com's initial branding as "the biggest bookstore in the world" – which has evolved into an online site with "the largest selection in the world" – but it also gives customers another reason to buy books through Amazon.

The program was created to provide faster book availability from independent publishers and more product listings for the site.

# LOCATION, LOCATION, LOCATION

Another Bezos innovation is his syndicated selling network. There are more than 60,000 commercial sites that help to sell books, and another 100,000 artist sites, fan sites, and label sites to help sell music and videos through Amazon.com. Customers want convenience, and a single mouse click may be the most convenient way to make a purchase today. Amazon.com has made it even more convenient to order books, by linking to other sites from which consumers may purchase from Amazon. For allowing the linkage, the sites get five to 15 percent of money from sales. Further, if location is a competitive advantage in retail, then Amazon.com certainly has this advantage, with its syndicated selling network of 160,000-plus sites from which consumers can buy products from the cyberstore. Through this network, Bezos now has an across-product program, enabling those who visit these associate sites, to purchase several titles across multiple product lines from a single source.

# CONSUMER CONVENIENCE

Besides destination sites, almost all Web search engines are members of the Associates Program. With hotlinks on each entry point and every research page, it's like Amazon.com has a store in each and every major mall in the world.

But customers don't just want a convenient place to shop; in today's busy times, they don't want to have to go to multiple stores to make their purchases, particularly if their purchasing needs are very similar in nature. So Bezos has increased the products he offers to his targeted customers. First it was books, then it was CDs, and shortly thereafter it was videos. Then during the 1998 holiday season Amazon.com added links to toy stores and computer stores, and offered comparison-shopping capability and links to various stores. His vision, he says, is "to accelerate access to things that inspire, educate, and entertain."

Thus Bezos' convenience strategy involves meeting multiple definitions of convenience, just as does Walgreens, which defines itself as a healthcare convenience and prescription business, and is one of the fastest-growing drug retailers in the US. It has over 2000 brick-and-mortar stores, and these stores are located not in malls but on the streets of cities and towns where they are easily accessible. More than 700 Walgreens stores have drive-through windows for prescription pickups and more than 400 are open 24 hours a day. Walgreens mail-order prescription business represents more than half a billion dollars.

As discussed in Chapter 3, on strategic focus, Amazon.com has another similarity to retailers. Retailers have to have a clear concept of their business – a precise definition of why customers should shop with them rather than competitors. They focus on the strategy and don't move from it. Walgreens sees it as maximum convenience for high-frequency shoppers. The Container Store sees it as solutions to storage and organization problems. The Home Depot sees it as building the do-it-yourself market, by teaching customers to undertake home projects rather than hiring someone else. Amazon.com sees it as offering "the world's largest selection." With the purchase of three European firms, Bezos announced his decision to expand beyond books to CDs and videos, as well as push to increase its overseas presence. The firms were: Bookpages Ltd, a small electronic bookstore in the UK, Internet Movie Database, a movie database that has supported Amazon's efforts to sell videos online, and Germany's ABC Telebook Inc., a German online bookseller. Bezos said of the purchases: "Visions do change over time. They expand."

In his purchase of three European firms, Bezos demonstrated his astuteness about the global market just awaiting Amazon.com. He set up Web sites in Germany and the United Kingdom (Amazon.de and Amazon.co.uk, respectively) and thereby he was able to reduce the cost of US book titles and their shipping time. Amazon.de is located alongside a distribution center in Regensburg, with editorial and marketing offices in Munich. It has over 350,000 titles from German publishers and speedy access to another 400,000 or so US titles. Amazon.co.uk is located alongside a distribution facility in Slough, England; it has a catalog of 12 million UK titles in print, fast access to 200,000 US titles, and speedy delivery. Both Web sites contain many of the customer features developed by Amazon.com: personalized recommendations, the ability to search for and locate books in a variety of ways, hundreds of browsing lists compiled by specific categories, reviews by experts and customers, and 1-Click™ ordering.

Bezos told *Success,* "We're not a stationary target. We were blessed with a two-year head start, and our goal is to increase that gap."

It would seem that Bezos is continually improving the systems, editorial content, and product offerings of Amazon.com – and with reason. The speed with which new companies come online and can make improvements in their offerings – both products and presentation – demands that companies continually reinvent themselves. While Amazon.com has several competitors on the Web, including an online Wal-Mart, investor attention is focused right now on its chief book competitor BarnesandNoble.com. Likewise, Bezos' attention seems to be on BarnesandNoble.com. As this online/real-time book chain aggressively moves to regain market share lost to Amazon.com, Bezos has had to respond. He has launched irreverent television and print advertising campaigns, purchased other companies with technology that give further reason for consumers to come to Amazon.com, and even entered into cross-branding, linking other sites to his own. It has been said that innovation-driven cultures exhibit a constant paranoia, continuously looking over their shoulder for competitors coming up on them, and Jim Clark, CEO of Netscape, has admitted that one of his primary responsibilities is to create paranoia. Bezos has mentioned such paranoia but he sees a problem in the obsession with competitors. Rather, the obsession should be with divining the future needs of customers and translating that information into innovations that give the firm a competitive edge. "Intel Chairman Andy Grove taught us all that only the paranoid survive, and he's right," Bezos said. "But the thing that drives everything is creating genuine value for customers. Nothing happens without that."

## KIDDIE SITE

An innovation that almost coincided with the entry of BarnesandNoble.com on the Web, was a special section of Amazon.com devoted to children's books. Most large bookstores have a special section devoted to such books, and Amazon.com is no different. In spring 1998, Amazon.com unveiled Amazon.com Kids, a one-stop kids' store within the Web site that offered a catalog of more than 100,000 book titles for children, teens, and parents. But Bezos knew better than simply to offer titles dedicated to children. So, as he has done with his adult books, he also has provided in-depth articles, reviews, interviews, and targeted search and recommendation services. Still not enough, the site includes new gift-ideas, recommendation and age-appropriate search engines. The Gift Ideas for Kids system is an interactive, fun-to-use system that enables customers to find the perfect book for the child who wants to grow up to be a doctor or a fireman, or become a performer on the stage, or play cowboys and Indians or space exploration, or read a mystery or teen romance. For family members who aren't sure about the suitability of a book for a specific age range, the selection service ties subject matter to age group.

Still another way Bezos has responded to BarnesandNoble.com's presence on the Web is to expand its distribution network by adding new distribution centers; earlier Amazon.com expanded the capacity of its Pennsylvania-based center to nearly six times its previous level and its Seattle warehouse by 70 percent. In addition to ease of ordering and discounting, another strength of Amazon.com is distribution – and it's a strength that Amazon.com intends to hold over its competitors. Most books are ordered from publishers or distributors, but Amazon.com clearly wants to increase its warehousing space to improve product flow of most frequently requested titles. Information on customer wants is data that the company can easily collect through its order technology. "Everything we do at Amazon.com is designed to continually enhance the shopping experience," Bezos has said, "and reducing delivery time does exactly that."

Shipping is a key issue in the catalog business, which is what Amazon.com really is, although the catalog is on the Internet.

Until late 1998, Amazon had two centers. In November, it opened its third center, on the west coast (Fernley, Nevada), to speed delivery in that part of the US.

In short, Bezos recognizes that quality service is a moving target. Once you satisfy customers in one area, their needs shift. You have to be alert to these changes and innovate or adapt to meet these new needs. That may mean acquisition and strategic alliances.

# BIBLIOGRAPHY

Anonymous (1998) "Amazon.com: the wild world of e-commerce," *Business Week*, December 14.

Gunther, Marc (1998) "Is competition closing in on amazon.com?" *Fortune*, November 9.

Hazleton, Lesley (1998) "Jeff Bezos: how he built a billion-dollar net worth before his company even turned a profit" *Success*, July.

Oliver, Richard (1999) *The Shape of Things to Come*, McGraw-Hill, New York.

Ten

# GROW WITH THE BEST

"If it's not growing, it's going to die."
**– Michael Eisner, CEO, Walt Disney Productions**

There are truly only three ways that Amazon.com will show profit:

1   Find new customers.

2   Increase the number of purchases per customer.

3   Increase the frequency of purchases.

Achievement of any or all three demand that the cyberstore give customers continuous reasons to come. Which means growth.

Today, the strategies for growth that organizations are using have changed – and Amazon.com's own expansion plan is evident of this.

In the past there were two choices: "buy" or "build." Organizations could either acquire another firm (via merger or acquisition) or they could build it themselves from scratch. Today, growth-minded organizations of all persuasions are not only acquiring businesses but also entering into partnerships or loose alliances to increase their opportunities for new product or service offerings and/or new markets.

# LOOK AT PARTNERSHIPS IN A NEW LIGHT

Since Jeff Bezos launched Amazon.com, he has used both acquisitions *and* strategic relationships to grow sales, improve services and bring in new custom. Two acquisitions have given Amazon.com a presence in Europe; another has provided the company with the capability to do comparison shopping on the Web; still another has given it the potential to remind customers about occasions for gift giving. A partnership in the cyber drugstore.com has given it another line of products – pharmaceuticals – to sell; still another will propel the site into the rare book business.

**Bezos on his purchase of Exchange.com: "It's a win for Amazon.com because it further increases our selection of rare and obscure items."**

Two further acquisitions are expected to simplify business-to-consumer transactions and to track which sites people visit and can make suggestions about other sites they might find interesting.

The site's home page has become cluttered as Amazon.com has added an online auction service and free e-mail greeting cards to its own inventory of books, CDs, and video tapes. And still more is expected. "Cards aren't going to be the last store you will see Amazon opening up," says David Risher, vice president of product development.

Through its Associates Program, Amazon.com has also signed syndicated selling agreements with over 100,000 independent sites, including multi-year exclusive or premier associate relationships with five of the top six sites on the Web: AOL.com, Yahoo!, Netscape, GeoCities, @HomeNetwork, and Alta Vista.

Via the program, individual sites select books they think will interest their own visitors, add their own reviews and recommendations, and then allow hotlinks directly to the Amazon.com catalog. Amazon.com takes care of business transactions, from securing online ordering to shipment, and then it provides weekly, automatically generated sales reports via e-mail.

There are also partnerships with independent book publishers under Amazon.com's Advantage Program.

## WHO LEADS GROWTH?

Whatever strategy a company takes to grow its business, the reality is that its leader has to take an active part in making it happen. When I first contemplated this book, I attempted to interview Jeff Bezos. At that time, I was told he was unavailable. What was he doing? His representative told me, "He was growing the business." Not only is it relevant that Bezos is consumed with growing Amazon.com but also that his staff all recognize that as his key responsibility. Bezos has built a culture that is looking to the future and focused on the possibilities of that future, not the constraints of either the past or the present. He has developed this attitude not only by role modeling attitudes toward risk taking and creating an environment in which employees aren't afraid to raise alternative ideas and propose new ways of doing things. But as earlier chapters of this book observe, Jeff Bezos has also made it a core aim to:

◆ Hire for growth. Members of Bezos' top team bring to their positions not only an understanding of e-commerce but a willingness to raise the bar both in the new industry they are personally helping to create and in level of service and variety of products specifically offered in the cyberstore. But within the employee ranks, too, Bezos also recognizes he needs those who can take ownership of problems and resolve them. Consequently, he has expanded his search for talent beyond typical types one would expect to find in ranks of a Web business, including former philosophy students among the BAs and MAs he is recruiting.

◆ Manage for growth. Sometimes growth occurs within existing divisions in a company through innovation; sometimes it occurs in the "white space" or what has been called organization orphans (that is, parts of the organization for which no part of the enterprise is yet responsive). The most flexible organizations are those that manage to get growth from both, using cross-functional teams where needed to pursue growth opportunities. Creating opportunities for sharing best practices is equally beneficial. Microsoft, for instance, keeps records about leaders of past projects and information from previous successes in a database filed by project and interest areas. This way anyone in need of help can retrieve the information and use it, sharing ideas and finding new best way to grow products and services. This process helps Microsoft respond quickly to ever-changing customer expectations. At Amazon.com, teams of employees work together on projects. The employees know that they can influence the success or failure of the business. "We're the ones who are going to make this company profitable," one employee reportedly told the press. And staff with the ability to impact Amazon.com's growth aren't only those who work on the Web site itself. Just the opposite.

While one immediately thinks about how exciting it would be to work on the software or information technology used at Amazon.com, operations is just as important, if not more so – it is certainly the largest part of the company. Bezos has grown his distribution network by adding two shipping facilities in the US, and facilities in the UK and Germany. All of them are located to minimize delivery time to overseas customers. Further growth is expected in this area over the next five years. "Operations" includes everything from identifying potential customers to building the Web stores limited inventory to getting shipments to customers, which means it includes all jobs in the company's warehouse and shipping centers. Operations can be thought of as Amazon.com's supply chain, and its Web site, as one insider has suggested, Amazon.com's advertising agency. Growth means giving management attention to both.

◆ Grow by a sense of community. If there is a new management buzzword, it would seem to be this one called "community." In reality building a sense of community, not only with employees by promoting a culture of trust and teamwork, but also with customers by aggressively seeking an ongoing relationship, is truly an effective way to build a company. The means by which community is created differ by industry. Airlines may offer various frequent-flier programs to induce passengers to use their company, whilst bookstores offer club members deeper discounts, and fast food restaurants offer regular customers "buy ten, get two more free" offers. At Amazon.com, an ongoing relationship is being built by personalizing service once enough is known about a visitor to make recommendations about new titles and favorite authors, and the like.

◆ Grow by being farsighted about customer expectations. No one could accuse Jeff Bezos of not working to stay aware of the ever-changing Web and the expectations, present and future, of visitors to Amazon.com. Indeed, this farsightedness about the next generation of customers – and generation after that – is what has prompted many of the partnerships of the past and is likely to influence future partnerships.

# HAVE PURPOSE IN YOUR PURCHASES

Each of the site's partnerships has had a purpose in keeping with the site's intention to offer "the world's largest selection." For instance, the cyberstore's own inventory of books numbers 4.5 million. Its acquisition of Exchange.com, which operates the Bibliofind and MusicFind Web sites, will add at least another nine million book titles. Acquisition of Accept.com, based in Redwood City, California, will provide the organization with solutions to simplify business-to-consumer transactions. Its purchase of Alexa Internet Inc., located in San Francisco, will enable the Webstore to track site visitors to its home page and make recommendations to viewers about other sites they might find interesting. It will also enable Amazon.com to gain data about regular visitors' interests to help grow business. To date, the company's services have sold to more than eight million people in the US and abroad.

Only three years after its launch, the company began to grow via acquisition. In 1998, it purchased Junglee Corporation, which had developed comparison-shopping technologies, thereby allowing Amazon.com to offer more than books, music, and videos to visitors to the site. That same year Bezos and his firm also purchased PlanetAll, an Internet site on which Web users could maintain their personal calendars and Web directories and had the potential of becoming a reminder service for Amazon.com to prompt customers to buy gifts for friends and relatives. Always in search of ways to provide added value to customers, Bezos saw PlanetAll with the potential to become one of the most important online applications.

## EXPAND GLOBALLY

As barriers have broken down between industries, so have the barriers due to distance. Companies are searching the globe not only for new suppliers but also for new markets. Amazon.com is no exception. It has recognized the need for a presence beyond the US borders and consequently launched Web sites in Germany and the UK, with the purchase of sites previously owned by ABC Bucherdienst in Germany and Bookpages Ltd in the UK. Amazon.com described the purchase as follows: "For the first time on a local basis, the sites make available to Europeans a vast selection, guaranteed safety of transactions, unparalleled convenience, and electronic gift certificates for worry-free gift giving." Visitors to these sites have access to the same services as available to customers of Amazon.com including:

◆ encryption for transmission of credit information over the Web

◆ personalization of services

◆ a variety of ways to search and locate titles

◆ hundreds of browsing lists compiled by specific categories of bestselling books

◆ reviews by experts and customers

◆ 1-Click™ ordering.

Even more important from a sales viewpoint, the sites abroad allow for a significant reduction in cost of shipment and delivery time for thousands upon thousands of US titles due to supply of the most popular American titles ready for immediate shipment from the UK and Germany.

On a global basis, Amazon.com has also signed an agreement with Yahoo! that makes them the premier book merchant for Yahoo's world sites, including Yahoo! in Asia, UK and Ireland, France, Germany, Denmark, Sweden, Norway, Canada, Australia and New Zealand, Japan, and Korea. The program was a global expansion of its existing relationship with Yahoo! Not only did the agreement with Yahoo! mean Amazon.com merchant buttons featured on Yahoo! Asia, Yahoo! France, Yahoo! Denmark, Yahoo! Norway, Yahoo! Sweden, and Yahoo! Australia and New Zealand, it gave Yahoo! Germany users access to a broad selection of German-language books from amazon.de and Yahoo! UK and Ireland users access to Amazon.co.uk's inventory of books.

## ALLY FOR A PURPOSE

Amazon's Associates Program or syndicated sales arrangement has meant banners and hotlinks on almost all of the most frequently visited search engines and hotlinks on over 100,000 more independent sites, from fan sites to corporate sites, to catalog stores on the Web. In return, the managements of these sites get a portion of revenue from sales via the hotlinks. For

Amazon.com, these links to other sites mean more traffic to the cyberstore. First-time visitors may make an impulse buy; if they don't buy, they may bookmark the site and come back at another time to make a purchase. The company's Advantage Program has given small independent producers of books and music, and tapes access to a major sales channel but it has also increased Amazon.com's inventory.

A review of these alliances illustrates a pattern. There are nine reasons why organizations join together, according to Mark N. Clemente and David S. Greenspan. Look at how these factors relate to Amazon.com:

> Despite attention on the Web site, operations is the largest area of the company. It's where we can see lots of growth in the next few years.

1   Effecting organization growth, which is clearly the overall goal of Bezos.
    Each of the ventures he has engaged in is intended to expand the number of offerings on the site to the kinds of offerings, to the kinds of services that will make customers want to come back.

2   Increasing market share, which entails a shift in customer loyalty from one enterprise to another. In Amazon.com's case, customers come from two sources: real-time and other Web sites that market the same products as it does. Strategic partnerships, whatever their nature, are designed to give customers reason to shift. So Amazon.com's acquisition of Exchange.com, the Associate Program agreements with Broadcast.com – from which Amazon.com will sell audio or video tapes – and Amazon.com's deal with Hoover Online which calls for Amazon to receive promotional

placements on Hoover's homepage as well as 13,500 on Hoover's Company Capsules, Hoover's IPO Central and Hoover's Online store, can all increase retail opportunities for Amazon.

3    Gaining entry into new markets or access to new distribution channels. Purchase of facilities in Germany and the UK have increased Amazon's access to markets in these two countries. Its purchase of warehouse facilities has meant safer and speedier delivery of orders. And its part ownership in drugstore.com has meant not only a new market but also new product line to market on the Web store.

4    Obtain new products. Since its launch in 1995, Amazon.com has increased its product offerings – from books to CDs to videos to computer hardware and software, and now to pharmaceuticals. At Amazon.com, you can either sell some collectible or other item, or buy something you had no idea you wanted until you saw it being auctioned at Amazon.com.

5    Keep pace with change. Amazon.com has continually re-invented the technology it uses to run its Web site and deliver quickly and safely product to customers. The timeframe in which the Web exists demands ongoing change, and Amazon.com has shown itself to be one of the businesses on the Web that sets the pace of technological developments.

6    Pursue innovations/discoveries in products or technologies. Acquisition of Junglee, PlanetAll, Accept.com and Alexa Resouces Inc. has helped the enterprise stay ahead of the

technological curve. The technology Amazon.com possesses allows it to track customer and potential customer interests. Then management has responded by adding new product and service offerings based on data accumulated. It also monitors competitive sites to determine similarities in customer demographics in traffic, and then looks at ways to bring that traffic to its site as well. Its decision, for instance, to offer visitors to the site the ability to send free cards to friends via the Web appears to be based on its observance of ever-growing traffic to Blue Mountain Arts. An article in *The New York Times* suggested that Bezos had tried to purchase Blue Mountain Arts. When he couldn't, he and his management team decided to build an equivalent service on their site, although Amazon.com's vice president of product development, David Risher, said the cards will be very different – "more playful offerings, including cards to celebrate holidays like Babe Ruth day." The goal is to encourage impulse purchase of a gift – from Amazon.com, of course – to go with the card.

7    Lessen competition. If you can't buy out a competitor, then you look for ways to strengthen yourself against the competition. Which explains Bezos' purchase of Exchange.com. The rare book company had also been courted by Barnes and Noble, Amazon.com's biggest competitor online and off.

8    Strengthen reputation or gain credibility. Each new offering of Amazon.com from purchase or partnership means more potential visitors to the Web site. To date, the company has had eight million customers worldwide. How many visitors or visits did it take to get these eight million customers? In my research, I was unable to determine a

figure on how many visitors Amazon.com has had over-all. But a chief information officer I know suggests that at present only a small percentage of visitors – sometimes as little as less than one percent – stay long enough at a site to make a purchase.

9   Respond to an economic scenario. The profitability of Amazon.com is based on an economic model that assumes x visitors of which y are customers or are likely to become customers. X is the critical number, and Bezos will con-tinue to grow the cyberstore to give the press reason to put the site in the news, advertise the site on radio and TV, and encourage those yet to visit the site to check it out, and previous visitors to return to check out the new services.

## CONDUCT DUE DILIGENCE

When you open the newspaper and see that Bezos has acquired or partnered with another business, it may make you wonder about the due diligence done prior to these acquisitions. I can't speak from any knowledge other than a respect for Jeff Bezos' leadership skills. Consequently, I assume that each and every acquisition or partnership was preceded by careful study of the organization bought or otherwise made a part of the Amazon.com community.

While advocating due diligence would seem equivalent to sup-port of baseball or motherhood on Mother's Day, many organizations limit due diligence to a study of a likely merger's bottom line. Little attention is given to its cultural or manage-ment fit or its market position relative to the acquirer. Should you find yourself in a position like Bezos and have to grow your business via acquisition or joint venture or other form of partnership, Clemente and Greenspan, in their book *Mergers & Acquisitions: The Guide to Market-Focused Planning and Integration*, recommend these, in addition to financials:

◆ Marketing investment ratios. Clemente and Greenspan say that the goal is to determine how much and how well money is invested in marketing – and the return for those past investments. This would seem to be of particular interest to someone like Bezos, who is continually looking himself for ways to enhance his company's brand.

◆ Efficiency ratios. You're looking here at operational efficiency. One measurement, for instance, might relate to customer satisfaction, another to staff turnover, still another to post-deal integration and growth planning. Again, this would be a logical issue for investigation by Bezos and his team given Amazon.com's own vigilance in regard to its expenses.

Breaking marketing issues down further, there are people issues. Clemente and Greenspan point out the need to measure the quality of marketing staff and sales force and the value they contribute to the marketing effort. "A strong and loyal customer base," they observe, "is even more critical, indicative of a firm that has successful programs to monitor and meet changing customer needs." You also have to measure a target company's relationship with distributors. In particular, you have to consider the impact of the merger on current ties. Finally, say Clemente and Greenspan, you have to determine if the organization as a whole is customer-centric rather than product-centric. "You want to target a company in which every employee is customer-focused and employees collaborate to meet customer requirements."

# CORPORATE GROWTH ALTERNATIVES

We shouldn't think about mergers and acquisitions as the only means toward an organization's growth other than build it yourself. There are many other choices available to an e-tailer or any other business, online or off, including:

◆ **Joint ventures.** This allows two or more businesses to pool their resources for a common gain. There are myriad strategic reasons for creating a start-up business, from developing new technology to commercializing products from new technology, to expansion in new markets. Some companies are expert at joint ventures, like Corning which has formed alliances with both tech and non-tech firms and has earned half of its income from joint ventures.

◆ **Strategic alliances.** Companies can choose to form strategic alliances to investigate technology or reduce individual expenses, to expand globally or otherwise explore new marketing opportunities, or increase distribution channels or improve supply chain management. The opportunities are limited only by the willingness of companies to ally with others, including competitors, to find new sources of revenue. Critical to their success are the same factors critical to joint ventures – common goals and values and minimal culture clashes.

◆ **Investments.** Larger companies can purchase minority positions in smaller businesses (e.g. Amazon.com's investment in drugstore.com), or they can provide venture capital for a business start-up. In the latter case, the investment allows the start-up to be run as an entrepreneurial business.

◆ **Licensing.** An enterprise may license another business to use a patent or a proprietary product or process. In return, it receives royalties from the license. For the company that licenses the product or process, licensing can mean minimal expense for access to a technology or product or process that cost its developer considerably.

◆ **Market agreements.** Such agreements can help companies widen the distribution of their products at least cost. Some companies enter into them because they lack experience about a region that the other party in the agreement possesses; others enter into such agreements because the other firm has specific strengths (e.g. distribution channels) and can do a better selling job.

◆ **Technology agreements.** The high cost of technology development has prompted companies to share their know-how and development costs. Bezos started his Web site by developing his own software. He still regularly reinvents the software he uses but he also acquires technology through acquisition of its creators' companies.

"Marketing due diligence," Clemente and Greenspan continue, "determines the extent to which the company's market share is sustainable and expandable." This means that those in search of a partner should consider brand power – name recognition coupled with positive market perceptions of product quality and value – and a target's level of innovation. "A company that regularly introduces new products and services brings value to the merger that one slow or ineffective in product introductions doesn't," say the two experts.

Consider one of Bezos' acquisitions against this Clemente/ Greenspan recommendation. They note that in acquiring other companies it is important to study the previous history of the potential acquisitions. One of Bezos' acquisitions, Exchange.com, was built by CEO Stig Leschly, primarily via acquisitions.

Look further at the acquisitions Bezos has made against this yardstick: Junglee and PlanetAll, and more recently Accept.com and Alexa Internet Inc. All are firms considered on the leading edge of technology.

Any company will have developed marketing and sales plans, but prospects for merger or acquisition, say Clemente and Greenspan, are those companies that actually achieve the goals in those plans on a regular basis. They note that management should look beyond short-term action plans to long-term corporate strategic plans. Further, they should study the bottom-line effectiveness of individual advertising, PR, direct mail, and other marketing communication. You are looking for a marketing department that consistently produces creative, sales-generating marketing campaigns.

Beyond this, you want a target company in which data relating to the firm's markets, customers, and competitors are regularly collected, and information systems are used not only to solve marketing problems but to support future initiatives, too. Internally, say Clemente and Greenspan, you are looking for channels of communication that directly support the company's sales and marketing efforts. "The more an organization imparts sales and marketing news, such as new product introductions and selling strategies, the greater the likelihood that it functions as a customer-focused organization across all levels and in all locations."

As I write this, I can't help but measure Amazon.com against these criteria. Clemente and Greenspan observe that these criteria make for a healthy organization, and I would argue that from a sales and marketing perspective Amazon.com would seem a well-run business. Not that I expect it to be acquired by another although there have been overtures (e.g. Bertelsmann who ultimately purchased a percentage of BarnesandNoble.com). But if you look at the criteria not as a measure of a firm to be acquired, but rather one poised for tremendous success, then Amazon.com would seem to be one.

But it is even more interesting how Amazon.com measures against Clemente's and Greenspan's management criteria:

◆ The company's leader. The experts in mergers say that the respect in which a CEO is held can have a tremendous impact on the final joining. As a leader, based on statements about Bezos by insiders, he has the respect of the members of his organization, as well as many, many investment managers and others breaking ground in this new thing called e-commerce.

◆ Management structure and culture. Executives who micromanage create an environment of distrust that diminishes productivity and increases fear of making mistakes and thereby decreases innovation and creativity in problem solving. Amazon.com's management would seem to support a risk taking culture in which employees feel they won't be questioned for every decision they make or have others looking over their shoulders.

◆ Level of teamwork and trust. Bezos has built a sense of community among Amazonians and he has built it around that dream he followed when, according to corporate folklore, he, his wife, and dog set out west to build a store on the Web. The story of that start-up was told and retold in many early press stories. More recent reports suggest a more organized, less fanciful start-up for Amazon.com. But this is irrelevant.

What is important is that the original idea of a cyberstore has been realized. Profitability will come in time. The only concern I have is that expectations are so great that no return will satisfy investors.

◆ Physical environment. Amazon believes in putting its money not in furniture but in customer satisfaction, brand enhancement, and technological developments. Consequently, this organization has never been known for its furnishings or other office trimmings. Not even corporate offices. Senior management hasn't had its ivory-tower quarter that distances it from employees. Consequently, the company has had, and would seem still to have, a relaxed, collegial environment.

◆ Corporate definition of success. Success is measured in various ways. If we measure Amazon.com solely on the basis of profits, I would have to say that it is yet a success. But if we use the yardsticks by which Bezos would seem to measure success – by risk taking, by technological innovation, by customer satisfaction, by a sense of community with employees – then we can say that in this investment phase *Amazon.com is a success.*

## GROWTH ON THE WEB

Jeff Bezos knows that it takes too long to "build for growth" on the Web. There is too little time in Web time to do so. Better to buy what you need or partner with another business – online or off – to provide the factors important to success.

Bezos demonstrates that in partnering with other firms he knows:

◆ Not to limit himself to acquisitions. There are other partnerships and agreements that Bezos has used to build the traffic to his site. His firm's agreements with five major search engines is a case in point.

◆ Build a culture receptive to partnerships. Bezos sees his role as creating a culture for growth, whatever it means. Consequently he not only role models the kind of attitude toward creative problem solving and risk taking he wants, but he also works hard to bring on board those who are willing to be empowered and make reasonable risks and take responsibility for solving problems.

◆ Have purpose in partnerships. Bezos would seem to be clear about what each partnership or acquisition is designed to accomplish for the fledgling cyberstore. Certainly a review of all the agreements and purchases over the last few years would make clear the contribution to the game plan each partnership is expected to make.

◆ Be farsighted about customer expectations. Data from the Web site provides lots of information about existing customers' wants and needs, and this information can be used to make decisions about how to take strategic plans further.

◆ Grow globally. Creation of operations abroad makes tremendous business sense, even if your store is virtual. Likewise, agreements like that with Yahoo! give Amazon.com hotlinks on every Yahoo! site around the world.

# BIBLIOGRAPHY

Anders, George (1999) "Amazon.com to add cards and rare books," *New York Times*, April 27.

Doler, Kathleen (1998) "Interview: Jeff Bezos: founder and CEO of Amazon.com Inc.," *Upside,* September.

Kotler, Philip (1999) *Kotler on Marketing: How to Create, Win and Dominate Markets*, Free press, New York.

Anonymous (1998) "The river wild: Amazon.com's recent acquisitions move it into new territory," *Red Herring Magazine,* November.

Clemente, Mark N. and Greenspan, David S. (1998) *Winning at Mergers and Acquisitions: The Guide to Market-Focused Planning and Integration*, John Wiley & Sons, New York.

# INDEX

Read on for more fascinating secrets about another digital giant, Michael Dell, the founder and CEO of Dell Computer Corporation.

The following pages are an extract from Rececca Saunders' *Business the Dell Way: secrets of the world's best computer company* published by Capstone Publishing in September 1999.

# From *Business the Dell Way:*
# *Secrets of the world's best*
# *computer business*
# by Rebecca Saunders

The "nerds" may be winners, as Tom Peters has declared, but they are winners not because of their lifelong love affair with technology but because of their entrepreneurial instincts – in particular, their ability to hold to a clear, compelling strategy. We have all heard about Bill Gates and we are increasingly learning about the management strategies of Webmeister Jeff Bezos, CEO and founder of Amazon.com. Another entrepreneur who has clearly defined the nature of the business and then tailored a system to ensure its successful implementation is Michael Dell, founder and CEO of Dell Computer Corporation. The organization that Dell heads is innovative, always searching for ways to improve the value of its products and to exceed customer expectations – and of course ways to adapt to the changing external environment – but in the process it has learned the value of staying with a single strategy: to sell direct to customers. By building computers tailored to customers' desires, often at below-retail prices, Dell has differentiated itself from other PC firms.

When Dell has strayed from this single focus, his business has suffered. In 1991, for instance, Dell Computer decided to expand beyond telemarketing to retail, selling through computer superstores and warehouse clubs. The numbers quickly prompted Dell to withdraw from retail.

*Success* noted that there are two kinds of entrepreneurs: "the deal junkies" who rush from one new venture or market to another, sometimes finding a pot of gold and oftentimes not, and "methodical optimizers," entrepreneurs who found a company based on a good idea and then build on that idea, constantly improving on it and, yes, adapting when the opportunities exist but never losing that strategic focus. Dell is the latter.

Most recently Dell has taken his idea of directly selling to customers on the Web, and sales at Dell's Web site now make up 50 percent of corporate business.

**Borrowing $1000 from his parents, Dell, then a freshman, sold computer accessories out of his dorm room.**

Most writers point to the start of Dell's business career in 1984 while he was an undergraduate at the University of Texas at Austin, but signs were already evident when at the age of 12, with a reseller's license, he conducted a nationwide mail-order stamp auction, making for himself a profit of $2000. Always interested in founding his own business, he sold subscriptions for a Houston newspaper. Dell told reporters that he realized that the majority of new subscribers were either new to Houston or recently married, so he researched new home purchases and marriage license applications at the county clerk's office to find prospects. "I sold a lot of newspapers," he recalls.

While studying biology in college, he recognized that computer sales involved drastic mark-ups by retailers who offered little service in the bargain. What cost a few hundred dollars in parts was being sold to consumers for several thousand dollars. A long-time computer hobbyist, Dell saw a niche and began to work it. Borrowing $1000 from his parents, Dell, then a freshman, sold computer accessories out of his dorm room. He would buy parts, assemble them into PC-upgrade kits, and then sell the finished products directly to customers. He was able to undersell far larger, more established competitors because he had eliminated the middle man who added little to the process except a substantial mark-up.

Soon after, he began to design and build his own line of computers. PCs Limited was making more than $50,000 per month when Dell chose to drop out of college. [Which was probably a good decision as he didn't do well on his final exams that year anyway, given the distraction.]

In 1988 he took the company public under the name Dell Computer Corporation. Around about that time, he also began to create the image of quality service that is associated with Dell. The company undertook the first on-site service program, which meant that consumers with sick computers didn't have to shlepp their computers to the local computer store for repair. Rather, Dell Computer came out to repair your machine. Dell had to do it this way – after all, the company had no stores to which computer purchasers could take their machines – but Dell's solution to his dilemma provided worthwhile value to customers, besides turning a corporate negative into a positive.

Dell Computer Corporation has grown from that simple beginning to become the second largest PC manufacturer in the US, with nearly 21,000 employees. As Dell shows signs of gaining on the leader of the pack, that leader, Compaq, has been prompted to emulate Dell, entering into the custom computer business itself.

What makes Dell's sales model so worthy of imitation? No need for maintaining large inventories of finished products or forecasting market demand in what is the highly volatile computer market. Dell builds computers only in response to real orders from end users – either by phone or now by Web site, which currently does around $6 million in sales every day. Computers are made in the firm's Austin factory where 1500 workers assemble the parts according to specific customer instructions and then test and box the computers for shipment – a process that takes about five hours. The business is international in scope, selling computers all over the world. Indeed, Dell was doing business beyond the US borders in the mid-1980s, way before many of the US giants then recognized the need to go global.

**Dell is the first to admit that his decision to sell directly to customers was prompted by necessity and not any great insights into the way business would move in the future.**

Dell is the first to admit that his decision to sell directly to customers was prompted by necessity and not any great insights into the way business would move in the future. "At the root of it," he has told the press, "I was opportunistic." On the other hand, Dell knew that he had a good thing when he found it and he hasn't swayed from "mass customization," which many industrial gurus regard as the paradigm for the next century. But concept isn't enough; businesses survive and thrive on execution and it is this that has earned Dell so many honors, like "Entrepreneur of the Year" from *Inc* magazine (1989), "Man of the Year" from *PC Magazine,* and "CEO of the Year" for 1993 by *Financial World* magazine.

*PC Laptop* magazine named Dell "Portable Pioneer" in 1994. Two years later, he was honored with the title "Best CEO of a

Turnaround" by *Upside Magazine* because of Dell's resurgence in the notebook market and success in the global markets. In 1997, he was included in *BusinessWeek*'s list of "The Top 25 Managers of the Year."

Wall Street marked Dell's executive leadership with the *Wall Street Transcript's* Gold Award in 1991 and its Silver Award in 1990.

What is behind all these managerial honors? Dell's success can be attributed to ten leadership secrets:

◆ **Secret #1: sell direct.** Dell eliminates the middleman by custom-building IBM clones and selling them directly to consumers, thereby reducing overhead costs and eliminating dealer markups. This is the original marketing concept behind Dell Computer.

◆ **Secret #2: value and manage inventory.** This is a direct consequence of Dell's sell and build approach to manufacture of PCs.

◆ **Secret #3: don't grow for growth's sake.** Dell learned this the hard way. In the second quarter of '93, Dell Computer experienced several expansion problems, including failure of a line of low-quality laptops. Growth is good, but it's controlled growth.

◆ **Secret #4: innovate or evaporate.** On the other hand, recognize that gradual improvements to each product line reduces risk and allows you to take advantage of rapid technological developments.

◆ **Secret #5: market innovate.** Dell was the first firm to market PCs by phone but $6 million in sales today comes from business off the Web. Be alert to opportunities outside of traditional distribution channels.

◆ **Secret #6: think and act global.** A young Dell Computer – and young Michael Dell – established the first of 12 international operations. He took his firm abroad almost a decade before most technology companies.

◆ **Secret #7: don't focus on computers, focus on customers and their needs.** Dell believes in going to where customers do business to understand their needs.

◆ **Secret #8: ally with employees.** Hire those who can generate ideas, train people to be creative, and create an environment that allows ideas to be tested.

◆ **Secret #9: ally with suppliers.** Highest quality comes from outsourcing manufacture of parts to suppliers with most expertise, experience, and quality in producing that part.

◆ **Secret #10: stay the course.** If the formula works, don't mess with it. Dell has been called a "methodical optimizer," someone who comes up with a good idea, recognizes it as such, then tirelessly pursues that idea, like sell and build and lean manufacture.

Want to know more? *Business the Dell Way* is published by Capstone Publishing in September 1999. Call 1-800-243-0138 in North America or +44 (0)1865 798623 outside North America for further details.